S J W s

ALWAYS DOUBLE DOWN

Books by Vox Day

Non fiction

SJWs Always Lie: Taking Down the Thought Police
SJWs Always Double Down: Anticipating the Thought Police
Cuckservative: How "Conservatives" Betrayed America
(with John Red Eagle)
On the Existence of Gods (with Dominic Saltarelli)
On the Question of Free Trade (with James D. Miller)
Return of the Great Depression
The Irrational Atheist

Arts of Dark and Light

Summa Elvetica: A Casuistry of the Elvish Controversy
A Throne of Bones
A Sea of Skulls

Quantum Mortis

A Man Disrupted (with Steve Rzasa)
Gravity Kills (with Steve Rzasa)
A Mind Programmed (with Jeff and Jean Sutton)

Eternal Warriors

The War in Heaven
The World in Shadow
The Wrath of Angels

Collections

The Altar of Hate
Riding the Red Horse Vol. 1 (ed. with Tom Kratman)

VOX DAY

SJWs

ALWAYS DOUBLE DOWN

CASTALIA HOUSE

SJWs Always Double Down: Anticipating the Thought Police

Vox Day

Published by Castalia House
Kouvola, Finland
www.castaliahouse.com

Cartoons: Gary "Redmeat" Kwapisz

Contents

Foreword

There are times when the age is dark, and men fill themselves with cynical despair.

There are also times when rare men step forth with unusual competence and shift the trajectory of the age in ways both seen and unseen.

Sometimes the work these men do is seen by the public. A highly successful musician, a nationally syndicated political columnist, a social media influencer reaching millions, or a bestselling philosophy author who sharply opposes the slide and crash of culture. These are all examples of sustained public effort and of leadership that has impact.

They are pillars of glittering prominence.

At other times, these important men are less visible but more deeply influential. They shepherd and mentor others to grow in their own crucial delivery. They run a publishing house. They educate others through lectures and debates. They provide counsel and support to those who run the gauntlet at the front of the cultural war while maintaining the calm and objectivity required of the mentor.

That is the work of men who place solid momentum ahead of ego.

In very unusual instances, these leaders may work silently in the background, forming ruthless cadres of smart and competent followers who carry out their work unheard and unheralded, shifting not just the trajectory of the age but the successes and failures of adversaries and allies alike in the darkness. This befits the mission of men who fight for their culture and civilization against those who do not follow the rules of honor. These are the men who will not surrender to the Adversary but protect and guard the light.

Vox Day is beyond rarity, for he has filled all of these roles.

And driven sharp success through each.

Appreciate this rarity, and listen.

SJWs Always Double Down is a gift, a bright lamp for us on the dark path of the cultural war in which we find ourselves.

Vox Day serves in many ways, in many milieus, and the hand of his work is rarely revealed across the arenas of contest. But there are times when it moves explicitly, and this book, *SJWs Always Double Down*, is a significant and essential contribution of truth, publicly declared.

There is no question that this is a tumultuous time of enormous cultural conflict and war, internecine and ugly, with no quarter asked and no mercy granted. The spoilt rejection of history and culture by the Left has directly, by design, methodically and cruelly destroyed intellectual integrity, political honor, sacred institutions such as marriage and the Church, and turned the emerging pillars and foundations of the digital age towards hideous outcomes of degeneracy.

Vox Day provided critical analysis of the character of the shrieking leftist in the first groundbreaking book of this series, *SJWs Always Lie*. He provided insight into the nature of the nasty inhabitants of the Left, their inability to adhere to truth—and very importantly, provided a survival guide to men and women suddenly faced with a merciless horde of social justice warriors determined to swarm and destroy them.

The next stage in competence against these destroyers is right here for you to study, to absorb, and to put into deliberate practice. With firmness, and competence, and consistent effort.

Today corporations topple, riddled with social justice warriors who screech and threaten and grovel, advancing by any means necessary their infected parasitism until the enterprise no longer exists to pursue its business in the market, but expires as a hollow husk, directed only towards the promotion of the social justice warrior ideology. All at the expense of the customers and markets it was built to serve.

This process is called "convergence," and it is the precursor to the eventual collapse and death of the enterprise.

This collapse and death is inevitable, for the parasitism of the social justice warrior is not symbiotic, but pervasive, destructive, and permits no preservation of value.

Vox Day unveils the workings of that process in this book and gives you the means to stop it with fire.

Even more disturbing today is concerted invasion of the open source community by social justice warriors of the Left, who seek to distract and corrupt an incredibly promising realm of innovation and technological growth by siphoning resources and time away from development of brilliant product.

The pathetic, pointless creation of "Safety Councils" and "Diversity Assurance Teams" corrodes, derails, and destroys the brilliance of digital group collaboration. These embedded cancers use shame, self-importance, and useless incompetence as tools of their metastasizing.

Vox Day exposes this draining assault on the vigor and coherence of the open source community as an example of deliberate social justice warfare, designed to turn the most brilliant endeavors of the day into hollow, failed husks inhabited only by humorless commissars.

The tactical instruction in *SJWs Always Double Down* is priceless.

But more importantly, this book drives home the reasons why this seemingly incomprehensible assault upon reason and performance keeps taking place, over and over again, despite the disasters that inevitably follow in its wake.

Why do social justice warriors not grasp that they bring businesses, institutions, ideologies, culture and civilization down to death, utterly heedless of the shouted warnings?

SJWs Always Double Down vivisects the compulsive and inescapable socio-sexual drives that lay behind the incomprehensible blindness of the social justice warrior.

Why are they so fatally parasitic, gobbling any and all available resources until the host who dares not fight back is dead and destroyed?

What causes their inherent blindness to objective, observable evidence that their conduct dooms and destroys everything it touches?

How can the social justice warrior declare victory at each and every failure after repeated failure and scorched earth demonstration of horrific incompetence?

Where can you interrupt this cycle?

How can you burn these swarms of the social justice warriors from the land as they double down on the total destruction of Western Civilization?

The answers are here, in *SJWs Always Double Down*.

Vox Day explains them in this book with the calm observation of a competent philosopher and the grim seriousness of the leader who does not seek aggrandizement, but victory against the dishonorable and destructive enemies of human reason.

See clearly where their evolutionary development has rendered them unable to refrain from lying, doubling down and projecting their own malevolently destructive worldview upon all others.

Learn why the self-annihilatory socio-sexual processes of the social justice warrior are inescapably rooted in their psyche.

Drive your understanding into the defense of not just your own reputation, career, safety and future… but also the survival and integrity of your company, your church, your institutions and your culture.

War without quarter is terrible, for men are crueler than all other beasts.

Losing war without quarter is worse because one cannot recover from it.

Vox Day wants you to win.

Vox Day is no longer just a social media avatar to me, a Supreme Dark Lord behind a Venetian mask.

Over the course of our work he has been a confidant and mentor, an ally and colleague, a standing remonstrance to those who despair and think it is too late to fight for the survival of Western civilization.

I have seen his loyalty to his friends, and it is both real and profound.

I have felt his calm and measured hand as it refined my own work, and it is deeply mature.

I stand here in my own right as a well-known combatant in the darkness of this age, and I tell you that it is an honor to introduce this important work to you, and to do so on the behalf of a man I consider a friend and a treasure to the West.

Read this book carefully, and read it well.

SJWs Always Double Down is your guide to survival on the battlefield of the cultural war.

That war is real and grows hotter with each day, and it will not be over until it has been won. It will not be over until we put an end to the myth of social justice and to the last misguided warrior who still believes in it.

Come join us in competence, in honor, and in the delight of a battle well worth fighting.

It is time to win, and this is the Way.

Ivan Throne
Colorado, U.S.A.

Introduction

A lot has changed in the two years since *SJWs Always Lie* appeared. Dozens of corporations and other organizations have been revealed to be SJW-converged. Hundreds of individuals have lost their jobs as a result of SJW attacks for reasons that would have been considered nonsensical only ten years ago. Tens of thousands more people are now aware of the existence of SJWs and of the vicious threat they pose to our friends, our families, our society, and even our civilization. But most people are still blithely unaware of them, and even if they have an inkling of their existence, tend to assume that they are impervious to SJW assault because they are good, well-meaning individuals. They find it difficult to believe that SJWs can really be as bad as they are portrayed and project their own good will and general lack of evil intent on them.

In most cases, it is not until a person is forced to directly confront the ugliness of SJW behavior, either in defense of his job or a pastime that he loves, that he is able to finally understand the reality of the situation. And when he does, he is often at a loss as to what to do or to understand with what sort of twisted, angry, psychologically damaged monster he is dealing.

This book is written to help that person understand, anticipate and defeat those monsters.

Before the reader delves into it, however, I should like to point out a few things about its predecessor, and respond to some common criticisms of it that may also apply to this book. First, I frequently use myself and the SJWs I have personally encountered as examples, not because I am narcissistic or settling any personal vendettas, but because those are the situations I know sufficiently well to describe in detail. Having actually been there, having witnessed the events, and being privy to all of the details both significant and incidental, those are the only situations I can definitively describe as having happened exactly the way they did. While it is reasonable to doubt whether I, as an active and interested party, can describe an incident in perfectly objective detail, it is worth noting that no one has dared to dispute or call into question any of the details of the various events I described in *SJWs Always Lie*.

A gentleman who not well-disposed towards me once said that although he disagrees with many of my opinions, he would not even bother to look out the window if I declared the sky was green. He recognizes, as do many of my friends, allies, and supporters, that I do not lie about things that can be objectively ascertained. The reason is that, since 2001, every word of the 500+ columns and 20,000+ posts I have written has been subject to intense scrutiny by hundreds of my most bitter opponents. I am well aware that this scrutiny exists, which is why even the most determined excavation into any aspect of this book or its predecessor will demonstrate that I am telling the truth to the full extent that I am able to do so.

Of course, this does not mean I will not engage in rhetoric or hyperbole from time to time, but the astute reader will recall that rhetoric is at its most effective when it is utilized in the service of the truth.

A second objection, ironically enough, is that I often delve into too much trivial detail when I am explaining a concept about SJW behavior through the use of examples. But this is absolutely un-avoidable because it is only in the examination of the minute details that the SJW devil can truly be seen with clarity. Due to the way in which SJWs habitually attempt to hide behind a fog of mutating definitions, move the goalposts without hesitation, and lie without shame, pinning them down in order to expose them usually requires a near-pedantic attention to detail. That being said, in this book I have attempted to more often demonstrate SJW behavior in their own words, by an extensive use of short, but illustrative, quotes in the place of lengthy, detailed descriptions on my part.

In much the same way that the great Carthaginian general Hannibal used his knowledge of Roman weaknesses and tendencies to anticipate them and to lead them into traps, we can use our knowledge of the SJW mindset and its patterns of behavior to create one metaphorical Cannae after another as we methodically obliterate their evil influence on our society. The advantage that we have over Hannibal, who despite his brilliance was ultimately defeated, is that this is our society and our civilization. We are the defenders, and like Fabius Maximus the Delayer, we need only refuse to surrender to them in order to eventually secure victory. They, not we, are the interlopers, and they, not we, have no claim on Western civilization, its values, and its traditions. They are the self-professed enemies of the West, and they seek its destruction, which is why there is ultimately no place for them in it.

I am occasionally asked why I am so implacably hostile to social justice. The reason is that I treasure truth, beauty, and God. Social justice places lies before the truth, ugliness before beauty, and Man before God. Social justice is not a good thing in any way, shape, or form; it is the antithesis of all that is good, and right, and true. It is evil, and therefore we must stand against it.

SJW delenda est.

Chapter 1

The Second Law of SJW

"What is Social Justice? Social Justice is the equal distribution of resources and opportunities, in which outside factors that categorize people are irrelevant."

—Pachamama Alliance

At last, your long ordeal at the hands of the corporate inquisition is finally over. After six months of being interrogated by suspicious HR managers, defending yourself against false accusations, clarifying all the intentional misunderstandings and mischaracterizations, explaining away the ridiculous exaggerations, and enduring the cold shoulder from half the employees in your office, your boss has assured you that everything is good and you are in the clear. You're grateful, of course, since he's been staunchly in your corner since the first time HR descended on you like a thunderbolt for your alleged sins against diversity and inclusion. In the end, it turned out that it was all the consequence of a Dilbert cartoon taped on the inside of your door, to which one of the women in the office took offense; at least, that was the only tangible offense that remained after the six-month investigation failed to turn up any evidence of all the other crimes of which you were accused.

"I really appreciate the way you went to bat for me," you tell your boss. And you're truly grateful to him. When everyone else looked the other way, happy that the wolves weren't out to devour them, your boss didn't hesitate to tell his superiors that all the rumors were ridiculous, even going so far as to provide a vice-president with your travel itinerary and proving that you were in Canada visiting customers on the day you supposedly lingered at the entrance of your nameless accuser's cubicle too long and made her feel uncomfortable. You're pretty sure that if it wasn't for him, you'd be out in the street looking for a new job already.

"Hey, you're a valuable member of the team," he assures you. "I'd hate to lose you, especially over some crazy nonsense like this. All you have to do is attend a one-day diversity class, and you can put this whole thing behind you."

Diversity class? But you didn't do anything! Didn't they just confirm that you didn't do anything?

"Why do I have to take the class now since they know I didn't do any of that stuff?"

He spreads his hands and shrugs. "You know how it is. Sure, everyone knows you're in the clear, but this lets the CEO assure everyone that we take racism and sexism and homophobia and all that very seriously, and keeps the directors off his back. I mean, the official story is that it's all just a big misunderstanding, right, so they're having you take this class to make sure there aren't any more misunderstandings in the future."

"But there wasn't any misunderstanding. It was all just a pack of outright lies!"

He winces. "Hey, I know that, and you know that. Hell, everyone in the executive suite knows that. But they can't come right out and say it either, can they?"

"Why not?"

"Because if they did, they'd have to fire the woman who brought the accusations against you, and nobody wants that kind of trouble. Look, we all know there is something seriously wrong with that woman. But if they fire her, we're talking a wrongful dismissal lawsuit at the very least, and probably other employees getting upset and threatening to quit, other whackjobs manufacturing sob stories about how they were harassed or offended or whatever, and HR going nuclear. And if word got out to the media that we fired a black woman, forget about it! By the time it was all over, we'd have to rehire her and promote her to department head, set up a scholarship fund for disadvantaged youth, and sponsor at least three Women in Tech conferences."

You stare at him, aghast. You can't believe that after putting you through six months of Hell for nothing, your accuser isn't going to get so much as a slap on the wrist.

"So that's it? I get eight hours of detention for doing nothing while she gets nothing for lying about me? Isn't there something in the employee handbook about not bearing false witness?"

"HR just thinks that's the Bible. It's not actually the real thing, you know." He laughs bitterly. "Blessed are the freaks, for they shall inherit the corner office."

So, with no little bitterness in your own heart, you heed his jaded advice and agree to do your time in diversity indoctrination camp. It's not so bad, really. It's essentially a day off, except instead of getting work done around the house, you're spending it being lectured by an angry Asian woman in power lesbian attire, a very fat white woman with blue hair who breaks down in tears every time she talks, and an effeminate, overweight black man in a dress whose posterior rivals that of a force-fed hippopotamus. It rather reminds you of college, actually, only the catered food is better and there isn't any beer.

Your fellow classmates are all white, all male, and most of them look bewildered and scared. They are programmers and IT guys for the most part, bearded and overweight and absolutely terrified of losing their jobs. The one exception to the general rule, besides you, is a thirty-something guy who looks like he might be from the Sales Department, a sharp-dressed fellow with an expensive haircut who smirks his way through the lectures, and occasionally bursts out laughing, much to the dismay of the inmates and the instructors alike.

"It's a good thing they finally brought the sandwiches," he says, after sitting down next to you during the lunch break. "The Blue Whale was getting hungry, and I think she was looking at you."

He's given them all nicknames. The Blue Whale. Caitlyn Kardashian. The Lesbotron (Made in China). He's kind of a riot, but you can't imagine his employment status surviving much longer.

"I suppose I don't need to ask you why you're here."

"Yeah, apparently I have been known to make hurtful and inappropriate comments. What are you in for, kid?"

"Dilbert cartoon."

"Oh, yeah? Which one!"

"The corporate politeness one."

"Ha! Now that's ironic."

Throughout the day, the Blue Whale and her sexually confused companions pontificate on the evils of society, the evils of men, the evils of the white race, and the horrific suffering their particular identity group has historically endured from the white male-dominated society formerly known as Western Civilization. One by one, each victim is encouraged to confess his sins against diversity and receive qualified absolution from one of the three minority figures, who increasingly strike you as an inclusive parody of the Three Fates. The Blue Whale spins a tale of how the guilty man's actions have harmed all womankind, Caitlyn Kardashian measures the depth of the offense in terms of its racism and Gay-Lesbian-Bi-Trans-Other-phobia, and the Lesbotron (Made in China) pronounces the sentence, which invariably amounts to some variation on her one-note theme of "the need to do better."

You dutifully go through the process, largely without incident, although it doesn't help when your new friend snickers after you stumble awkwardly over the phrase "the intertextual implications of my white male privilege." No harm is done, though, as the Lesbotron (Made in China) contents herself with shooting eye-daggers at him and accepts your ritual apology after you promise to Do Better and Be More Aware and Check Your Privilege.

Even the sales guy performs the ceremonial abasement, so smoothly that if you hadn't been privy to his earlier comments, you would have sworn his remorse was heartfelt and sincere. After a teary hug from the Whale, a fist-bump from the Kardashian, and an acidic benediction from the Lesbotron (Made in China), your collective reeducation is finally deemed complete and you are given permission to go forth and sin no more against the dark-skinned, the downtrodden, and the disprivileged of the world.

In the parking lot, you exchange cards with a few of your fellow parolees and are not at all surprised to discover that your new friend is driving a late-model Mercedes. You shake his hand and find yourself a little taken aback by his uncharacteristically serious tone when he gives you an unexpected warning.

"Be careful out there," he says, which you feel is a little incongruous, considering that it comes from him, of all people. "You'd better watch your back."

"Me?" You were rather pleased to discover that your unapproved cartoon was the most innocuous of all the various crimes against diversity that had been committed by that rough gang of white male privileged thugs, so you wonder why you're the one who needs to be careful. It's not as if you're prone to unconsciously cutting things out of the cafeteria newspaper in your sleep, after all. You might be a man of modest and limited talents, but you are fairly confident that not posting any more Dilbert cartoons in your cubicle, or indeed, anywhere in the office, is well within your range of capabilities.

"They had you in there for nothing. I mean, Dilbert? Come on! That means someone with influence wants you gone. Not for what you did, but for who you are."

"Me? Why?"

"I have no idea. But I guarantee you someone is after you, and she's not going to quit either."

"That doesn't make any sense!"

"Who said it had to? Maybe someone wants your job? Nah, you're just a cubicle jockey. Look, you obviously pissed someone off, and I can tell you this: she is not going to stop coming after you. She'll be like the Terminator, man. You look at her the wrong way, you sneeze when you should have coughed, and she'll be running to HR shrieking about how you killed her and raped her, used the N-word and the other N-word, then microaggressed her by asking where she's from."

"The other N-word?"

He laughs. "If you don't know, more power to you."

"What's the matter with asking someone where he's from? They didn't mention that today."

"That's offensive, my man. Do try to keep up. See, if you notice they're from somewhere else, then you're implying that you believe they don't belong here. Could you be more racist?"

"So we just shouldn't notice anything?"

"Exactly!" he beams at you and then puts a hand on your shoulder. "You see, my friend, your problem is that you're in a war and you don't even know it. You've got to learn to duck when they're shooting at you, or sooner or later, you're going to get shot in the head."

You assume he's speaking metaphorically, although at this point, you're not entirely sure. "You don't seriously believe someone could get fired over a stupid cartoon, do you?"

He only laughs and points to a little bearded man getting into a Prius. You recognize the guy. He was one of the programmer types who seemed particularly shaken by being forced to attend the class and intimidated into near-speechlessness by the Three Diversities.

"Know who that is?"

"No, should I?"

"Well, your job probably depends on him. He's the lead programmer for the team writing the core engine for version three."

You look at him in astonishment. You're not in sales, but you know that version three is what will make or break next year for the company. It's already six months late, and most of the major clients are impatiently waiting for it. What on Earth are the executives doing letting that guy out of his cubicle, at all, let alone making him waste an entire day like this?

"Does Jack know he was here?" Jack is the CEO.

"Jack probably knows what that guy had for breakfast and how many times he went to the bathroom yesterday. He's been breathing down the poor guy's neck for the last nine months."

"Then what's he doing here?"

"You just don't get it, do you? Jack's scared of HR. Everybody in your company is. If HR says some weird little guy has to sit through a day of cultural reeducation because he stared at a pretty intern from Stanford for one too many seconds, then Jack isn't going to tell them no. He knows that if he doesn't give the psychopaths in HR whatever scalp they demand, it won't be long before they go after his. He's a straight white guy, just like you. If he doesn't play ball, the next thing he knows, he'll be facing three sexual harassment lawsuits, and every other article about the company will say that it isn't taking inclusion and Women in Tech seriously, and suggesting that its time for a diversity CEO."

"Oh, God."

He's right, you realize. He's absolutely right. Jack isn't in control. Jack is riding the HR tiger, and he's terrified of falling off. Then something that he said strikes you as incongruous.

"You just said 'your company'. Not our company. Do you even work here?"

He grins. "Not even a little bit."

"Then what on Earth were you doing there?"

"Research." He laughs as you gape at him and produces a card. You recognize the name of the firm for which he works. It's one of the more successful tech-focused hedge funds. "When we're making ten-million-dollar bets on a company we like to know what we're betting on."

"So you just crash these re-education courses?"

"You'd be amazed at what you can learn from what a company believes to be a disciplinary infraction." He waves in the general direction that Prius Guy departed. "I'd say today was a very good use of my time."

"What do you do if you get caught?"

He laughs again. "I tell them I'm with the Anti-Defamation League, verifying that the company's Diversity and Inclusion program is fully consistent with what the ADL has determined to be corporate best practices."

"Does that work?"

"Every single time. You should see them freak out when I criticize them for being out of date on the LGGBDTTTIQQAAPP front."

"The what?" You gape at him, astonished.

"It's what used to be LGBT. Now it's Lesbian, Gay, Genderqueer, Bisexual, Demisexual, Transgender, Transsexual, Twospirit, Intersex, Queer, Questioning, Asexual, Allies, Pansexual, Polyamorous. Leave one out, you're a hater, don't you know?"

"No. You've got to be making that up!"

"I think the Twospirit thing is only in Canada for now, but other-wise, no, it's really that crazy. Once I even got offered a job as VP of D&I."

"Really?"

"Well, I told them I was gay and Jewish. Given how well I speak Diversity, you could hardly expect them to resist."

You laugh. Then you frown. "So, I suppose you're thinking that it doesn't look too good for us."

"No, not at all. I just wish you guys were public so we could short the begeezus out of you. My guess is that you'll be a takeover target within six months at a valuation less than half what everyone thinks now. Thirty-five, forty percent tops."

"A takeover?" You shrug. "It could be worse."

"Sure, except you can bet that your management team will be announcing mass layoffs right around the time they have to push back the release date. And unless I miss my bet, you, my friend, are already on HR's hit list. Someone doesn't like you. Just because you escaped the guillotine once doesn't mean they're going to give up and leave you alone. Ever play poker?"

"A little, yeah."

"When do you double down on a bet?"

You frown. And then suddenly the answer becomes clear to you. He smiles at the expression on your face. He sees that you're finally starting to get it.

"Right. It's not when you're think you're going to win. It's when you're sure that you can't lose."

"So what you're saying is, I'm screwed."

"I'd say it's time to polish that résumé and get it circulating. And you'd better learn to duck and cover, my friend. Considering your line of work, it's not going to be any different at your new job. You survive long enough, maybe then you can figure out how to shoot back at the bastards."

Whether you realize it or not, if you live in the West, you are currently engulfed in a civilization-wide cultural war that is taking place all around you. Maybe you're aware of it, or maybe you're not. It doesn't matter. The cultural war is real and it is vicious. And unlike a traditional shooting war between different nations, in a cultural war there are no civilians. There are no neutral parties since no fence-sitting is permitted, and there is no common ground to be found. No one is permitted to sit it out or refuse to take sides; sooner or later, you are going to be forced to declare yourself by either publicly submitting to the SJW Narrative or openly rejecting it.

Don't think that you're the first to pride yourself on being open minded, on being friends with those with whom you disagree. Don't deceive yourself into thinking that because you don't insist that everyone agree with you, that will render you off-limits to those who insist that everyone has to agree with them. Don't flatter yourself that you are different or special in any way or that your cross-spectrum friendships are any stronger than anyone else's. And above all, don't think that you are bulletproof simply because you are intelligent, famous, rich, popular, accomplished or important to the organization.

Not even belonging to one of the disadvantaged categories is going to protect you if, for one reason or another, you frighten too many SJWs by successfully defying their holy Narrative.

It's not about you.

That's what you have to understand. It's not about you; it's all about them. You're just the target du jour, the trophy to be taken.

I wasn't too intelligent, or too Native American, to be targeted by the SJWs in science fiction. Daryush Valizadeh wasn't too Muslim or too immigrant, and Milo Yiannopoulos wasn't too famous, or too charming, or too gay, to be targeted by media SJWs. Brendan Eich wasn't too important to Mozilla, and Larry Garfield wasn't too important to Drupal, to be targeted by tech SJWs. PWR BTTM was not too artsy-fartsy and genderqueer to be targeted by music SJWs. The Nobel Laureates James Watson and Sir Timothy Hunt were not too accomplished to be targeted by science SJWs. James Damore wasn't too innocent and well-intentioned to be jettisoned by the SJWs at Google.

No matter what you do, no matter who you are, and no matter who you know, the SJWs will come after you once they believe you pose a threat to their Narrative, or to their objectives for the organization. But that is not the only reason they identify and attack people.

They have also been known to do so in order to burnish their SJW credentials; the more sensitive to microaggressions and badthought and crimespeak they are, the higher they rank in the SJW hierarchy. Leading the takedown of a well-known individual for his crimes against social justice is the ultimate trophy for an SJW. They will also target those who are in positions of tactical and strategic importance in the organization they are invading; SJWs always gravitate towards HR, corporate boards, and compliance committees in order to wield influence over who is allowed entry into the organization and who is driven out of it.

And, as many people have discovered in the aftermath of the U.S. presidential election, SJWs will even attack those whose mere existence triggers their negative emotions. An employee at Google was fired from his job only a few weeks after the election on entirely spurious grounds; the real reason was that his co-workers discovered that he had voted for Donald Trump and were infuriated by that knowledge. Being a heavily converged company, Google employees were openly attacking other Googlers for being racist, sexist, and homophobes simply because they voted for the winning Republican candidate. Since racism, sexism, and homophobia are firing offenses at Google, the SJWs there were implicitly declaring that no one who voted for Donald Trump should be permitted to work at Google.

That's a remarkably extreme position, considering that 62,979,879 people voted for President Trump, who won the Electoral College 304 to 227, won 30 out of 50 states, and won 2,623 of the 3,112 counties in the United States.

The point, in case it is not yet sufficiently clear, is that no matter who you are, it is utterly foolish to expect to be able to reason, compromise, negotiate, or coexist with an SJW. Even if you erroneously believe you have somehow managed to reach a functional accommodation with an SJW, it will only last until you happen to cross one of the ever-shifting lines of the Narrative, or some event external to your relationship triggers them, and thereby causes them to turn on you. Any relationship, be it personal, professional, or romantic, with an SJW is intrinsically unstable; you might as reasonably expect to cuddle with a wild wolverine. Sooner or later, for one reason or another, the damned thing is going to attempt to claw your insides out.

It's very difficult for a normal individual to grasp the extreme instability and emotional intensity of the average SJW. The reason is that social justice is not actually a political phenomenon, even though most of its actions and language revolve around nominally political issues. Social justice is, at its core, a quasi-religious ideological cult posing as a philosophical imperative, an ideological cult that comes complete with its own morality, even if that moral system is more flexible than an Olympic gymnast and more prone to mutating than *E. coli* in a scientific researcher's lab.

I know some of my friends have wondered why I've lately been so critical of the left, my home, so I wanted to share with you what a vocal part of my particular and admittedly self-selected echo chamber is like.... The ideology is post-modernist cultural marxism, and it operates as a secular religion. Most are indoctrinated in liberal elite colleges, though many are being indoctrinated online these days. It has its own dogma and jargon, meant to make you feel like a good person, and used to lecture others on their 'sin.' "Check your privilege"—much like "mansplaining" and "gaslighting"—all at one time useful terms—have over time lost a lot of their meaning. These days I see them most frequently being abused as weaponized ad hominem attacks on a person's immutable identity markers... a way to avoid making an argument, while simultaneously claiming an unearned moral highground in a discussion. I have been wondering why more people on the left are not speaking up against violence, in favor of free exchange of ideas and dialogue, in favor of compassion. But I know why. I was in the cult. Part of it is that you are a true believer, and part of it is that you are fearful of being called an apostate—in being trashed as a sexist, racist, homophobic, transphobic, Islamophobic, xenophobic, fascist, white supremacist nazi.

> —"On Leaving the SJW Cult and Finding Myself",
> Keri Smith, 13 May 2017

The SJWs, or Social Justice Warriors, did not give themselves that name in any ironic sense. They called themselves that because they genuinely consider themselves to be crusaders fighting for the righteous cause of creating a new and better world, one in which every individual and organization will be fully dedicated to social justice ideals.

And as for those who refuse to dedicate themselves to social justice, there will be no place for them in the brave new world of the SJW.

That doesn't sound so bad, perhaps, to those for whom there is no longer any place in their former university, open source project, Fortune 500 corporation, church, or social club. Except the problem is that SJWs seriously intend to leave no place anywhere in the world for those who reject their Narrative and refuse to abandon their outmoded, outdated, problematic ideals that have been superseded by social justice. As Virginia Governor Terry McCauliffe publicly declared in the wake of the Unite the Right rally in Charlottesville, "There is no place for you here, and there is no place for you in America."

Where, then, is the non-SJW to go? What, then, is the non-SJW to do?

My suggestion is to fight back. To fight back and win. Because, in an SJW-converged world, there is no place for anyone who has not submitted completely to the SJW Narrative. Even Islam is more tolerant.

There can be only one.

Chapter 2

Peak SJW and the Backlash of 2016

It is a good rule in life never to apologise. The right sort of people do not want apologies, and the wrong sort take a mean advantage of them.

—P.G. Wodehouse

Prospects for a better world and a global society of true equality had never looked brighter to the intrepid warriors of social justice than they did at the end of 2015. The culmination of a 165-year campaign to transform a white Christian West into the shiny, secular, nonjudgmental, socially just society of John Stuart Mill's dreams increasingly appeared to be inevitable. Even if the total convergence of every individual and every Western institution towards social justice had not yet come to pass, SJWs were brimming with confidence that the point of no return had been passed. Numerous academics and political activists celebrated each and every signpost indicating the decline of America's white majority. Journalists and atheists greeted each published poll indicating fewer church-attending Christians than there were in previous years with glee. For the first time in American history, men were legally permitted to "marry" men, women were permitted to "marry" women, and the academics announced that sex was not a biological reality, as so many had previously believed, but a mere social construct.

And if the world never looked brighter to the SJWs, it had seldom appeared darker or more hopeless to the defenders of traditional

Western civilization. It seemed that after 80 years, Antonio Gramsci's long march through the cultural institutions of the West was finally complete and that everything from the Boy Scouts to the Roman Catholic Church had been successfully converged. Consider a few of the recent cultural lowlights:

- *Boy Scouts of America Amends Adult Leadership Policy. On Monday, July 27, the National Executive Board ratified a resolution that removes the national restriction on openly gay adult leaders and employees. Of those present and voting, 79 percent voted in favor of the resolution. The resolution was recommended for ratification by the Executive Committee earlier this month. The resolution is effective immediately.*

- *The Army's Cadet Command at Fort Knox, Kentucky, is reviewing Reserve Officer Training Command cadet participation in a sexual assault awareness 5K walk/run event in which cadets at Temple University in Philadelphia wore high-heeled shoes with their uniforms.*

- *In a historic transformation of the American military, Defense Secretary Ashton B. Carter said on Thursday that the Pentagon would open all combat jobs to women. "There will be no exceptions," Mr. Carter said at a news conference. He added, "They'll be allowed to drive tanks, fire mortars, and lead infantry soldiers into combat. They'll be able to serve as Army Rangers and Green Berets, Navy SEALs, Marine Corps infantry, Air Force parajumpers and everything else that was previously open only to men."*

- *Pope Francis calls on every parish across Europe to house refugee families. The pontiff specified the scope of his request: "Every parish, every religious community, every monastery, every shrine of Europe house a family, starting from my diocese of Rome... Often we are withdrawn and closed in ourselves and we create many inaccessible and inhospitable islands. So much so that the most basic human*

relations at times are created from reality unable to make reciprocal
openness: the closed couple, the closed family, the closed group, the
closed parish, the closed homeland. This is not from God! This is
ours; this is our sin."

- *The Majority of American Babies Are Now Minorities. Racial and*
  ethnic minorities now surpass non-Hispanic whites as the largest
  group of American children under 5 years old, the Census Bureau
  said Thursday.

- *"Caitlyn Jenner: The Full Story". Few recent stories have gripped the*
  public imagination as much as Bruce Jenner's journey from Olympic
  icon to transgender woman.

Perhaps the pinnacle of the social justice peak of 2015 was when
German Chancellor Angela Merkel publicly announced that Germany
would welcome an unlimited number of refugees from Syria,
prompting a one-million-strong horde that hailed from every Muslim
country in Africa and the Middle East to invade Europe in the hopes
of tapping into the generous German welfare system. The end of the
evil, imperialist Christian West and all its terrible works appeared to
be at hand. At last, every institution and individual appeared to be
converging towards social justice in the manner envisioned by John
Stuart Mill.

But all was not quite as it seemed.

Whereas 2015 marked the peak of SJW power and influence across
the West, the inevitable backlash in 2016 demonstrated that the
nations, institutions, and people of the West were not fully converged.

The overturning of the SJW apple cart that took place in 2016 had
its roots in events taking place four years before. In 2012, there was
a rebellious mood permeating the grass roots of the Republican party.
Eight years of so-called compassionate conservatism, which turned
out to be little more than permitting neocons to run U.S. foreign
policy while the Bush administration continued domestic and trade

policies that were all but indistinguishable from Bill Clinton's, had been followed by the inept campaign of Republican moderate John McCain. McCain's self-imposed implosion—he had shut down his presidential campaign in order to rush to Washington D.C. to help funnel billions of dollars to his banker buddies—cost him 6 points in the polls, and a month later, the presidential election of 2008. But when Ron Paul, the iconoclastic Congressman from Texas, began to show unexpected strength against Mitt Romney, the moderate candidate favored by the establishment Republicans, the party insiders pulled out all the stops to shut down his upstart campaign and to silence his enthusiastic supporters.

The stage was further set by eight years of the Obama administration, during which time even the gentlest criticism of the President of the United States was immediately met by a hailstorm of accusations that the critic was a racist, a hater, and quite possibly a member of the Ku Klux Klan. As one social media wag, Jon Gabriel, dryly observed: "My favorite part about the Obama era is all the racial healing." Nor did it help that the technology giants, including Facebook, Google, Intel, and Apple, were increasingly bowing to SJW pressure to increase diversity and perversity while suppressing anyone who dared to question, let alone protest, their ongoing convergence. Twitter even went so far as to set up the Orwellian-sounding Trust and Safety Council and bragged about shutting down more than 500,000 accounts on the basis of them expressing impure thoughts. And the 538 thought police of Wikipedia continued to crack down on every editor who dared stray from the SJW narrative on their online encyclopedia, no matter how obscure the topic.

SJWs were not so much confident that victory was in sight as certain that it has already been won. They looked on the election of Hillary Clinton as the first female President of the United States as the spiking of the football in the end zone after the winning score and as a prelude to the mopping-up operation that would render traditional white reactionary America as harmless as the post-Reconstruction Confederacy.

But the first sign that current events were not entirely in line with the social justice Narrative duly reported by the media on a daily basis was when Donald Trump, who had previously been regarded as little more than a buffoonish celebrity joke-candidate, won the South Carolina Republican presidential primary. While his previous victory in New Hampshire had been dismissed as the same sort of aberration that, 20 years before, had resulted in a victory by conservative commentator Pat Buchanan, Trump's resounding victory in South Carolina made it obvious to those with the eyes to see that something out of the ordinary was taking place. And in due course, against the expectations of literally all the professional political pundits, Donald Trump went on to win the Super Tuesday primaries, the Republican nomination, and eventually, the U.S. Presidency as well.

The second sign was when the British, who had endured their own foreign invasion for decades, unexpectedly voted in a national referendum to leave the European Union. In voting Leave, the British people defied their own government, all three of their major political parties, the BBC, most of the daily newspapers, most of the economic experts, most of the European heads of state, celebrities, the U.S. President, and, of course, the predictions of the pollsters. Not only did they support what had come to be known as Brexit, but in doing so, they also forced the resignation of the anti-Brexit Prime Minister, David Cameron.

The third sign was when the Italian people, in what amounted to a de facto referendum on the pro-EU administration of Italian Prime Minister Matteo Renzi, rejected a proposal to amend the Italian Constitution to reform the composition and powers of the national parliament and to alter the division of powers between the central Italian government and the regional governments. The proposal was abandoned, and a humiliated Renzi followed his British counterpart's lead by resigning.

Taken together, these three democratic expressions of the will of the people in the United States, the United Kingdom, and Italy made it eminently clear to even the most rabid advocate of global social justice that the SJW Narrative was false and that neither social justice ideals nor the converged society were popular with the majority of the people of any nation despite the unrelenting SJW propaganda to which they had been subjected. This discovery came as a complete shock to SJWs both low and high, as the only thing more astonishing to them than the unexpected success of the Brexit Leave campaign in the United Kingdom was Donald Trump's subsequent 304-227 Electoral College victory over Hillary Clinton in the U.S. Presidential Election.

Virtually no one expected the ascension of the cheesy 1980s financial celebrity to the Oval Office. We were assured, repeatedly, every step along the way, that Donald Trump's campaign had reached its apex and that while Trump might have exceeded initial expectations, his inevitable doom was right at hand. The following are a list of public predictions made by professional political observers, each and every single one of which proved to be false.

- Trump will never run for President.

- Trump will never breach 15 percent.

- Trump will never win New Hampshire.

- Trump will never release his financials.

- Trump will never breach 25 percent.

- Trump will never win South Carolina.

- Trump will never breach 35 percent.

- Trump will never breach 50 percent.

- Trump will never reach 1,237 delegates.
- Trump will never recover after losing Wisconsin.
- Trump will never win unbound delegates.
- Trump will never recover after losing Colorado.
- Trump will never be embraced by conservatives.
- Trump will never be the Republican nominee.
- Trump will never win the swing states of Florida, North Carolina, and Pennsylvania.
- Trump will never win the U.S. Presidential election.

There were a few, a very few, observers who did correctly foresee Donald Trump's election. As it happens, along with Mike Cernovich and Scott Adams, I was one of them, as this post from December 9, 2015 should suffice to demonstrate.

In this electoral campaign cycle, Trump is the only candidate who matters, and it is not because of who he is or what he might do if he wins. This is basic game theory. As I have said repeatedly in the past, there are only three issues that matter today. In their current order of importance, they are: Immigration, Gun Control, and the Federal Reserve.

We can ignore the latter. None of the candidates even understand the issue and none of them are likely to do anything about it. Trump, being a maverick, is the only one who might even look at the issue, but that's totally speculative and therefore irrelevant.

On guns, Clinton and Sanders are terrible, Ben Carson is bad, and most of the Republicans, including Trump, are both good and reliable.... That leaves immigration. And here, Trump is the only candidate who is even beginning to address the scope of the existential

*problem. All the Democrats, and more than half of the Republicans,
actually want to make it worse. Even if you don't support him,
or trust him, the mere fact that he is in the race has changed the
debate on the subject more than the combined efforts of every anti-
immigrationist, every open-borders skeptic, and every anti-free trade
economist. He has been a literal Godsend in this regard, no matter
what happens in the end.*

*In short, Donald Trump has radically changed the culture, and
culture always trumps politics.*

Seven months later, I wrote an article called "The Trumpslide
cometh." Four months after that, on the eve of the election, I was
increasingly confident that Trump was going to win, even though
nearly every poll in the country had Hillary Clinton winning both
the popular vote and the Electoral College, with the exception of
the *Investor's Business Daily* national poll. This was notable because
IBD/TIPP had been the most accurate presidential poll since 2004.
But pollsters are, by and large, SJWs, and we all know what SJWs
always do. From overloading the percentage of Democrats in their
polls to focusing on registered voters rather than likely voters, the
pollsters make a profession of putting a thumb on the scale in order
to try to bring about the end result desired by the media. Even those
pollsters who are not SJWs are primarily employed by the media,
and so it should come as no surprise that they show a reliable tendency to shade the truth in the direction preferred by those who pay
them.

But the more reliably deceit is committed, the easier it is to recognize the pattern of deception. What the polls could not hide, despite
the media's best efforts, was that the trend was towards Trump. This
is because, in order to keep its manipulated poll results sufficiently in
line with the actual vote to maintain a degree of future credibility, the

polls have to gradually reduce the amount of false support they are inventing for the preferred side. To cover for this, the media customarily reports that "the race is tightening" and "previously undecided voters are making up their minds," although both excuses are nonsensical, particularly in the case of the 2016 U.S. presidential election.

The latest—perhaps even final—Real Clear Politics No Toss Up States map has Hillary Clinton hanging on by her blood-stained fingernails, 272-266. Long vanished are all the claims of an easy Clinton win, which, as I have repeatedly stated, were complete fiction from the start. Trump only needs to take ONE toss up state they've given her from the following list of six to win: NH, PA, MI, CO, NM, VA. Of these, I think New Hampshire and Pennsylvania are the most likely. I think he'll take both, and Michigan and Colorado as well. Meanwhile, several Minnesotans have told me, in all seriousness, that they expect Trump to take Minnesota. I find that almost impossible to believe, considering that Minnesota has historically been the most reliably Democratic state in the country, but people are extremely unhappy about losing Dinkytown to the Somalis and the Mall of America to the blacks, and about the St. Cloud mall stabbings.

As the exit polls came in and the media started calling states for one candidate or the other, it soon became clear that if Donald Trump managed to win Florida, he would win the election. At 9:43 PM EST, I observed that with 523 of 577 precincts reported in Broward and 797,624 ballots counted. Trump still led by 132,000 votes. This was important because Broward County is very large, dominated by shameless Democrats, and notorious for belatedly producing "missing ballots" that are magically discovered after other Florida counties have reported their results and the county officials learn how many ballots they need to "find" in order to push their candidate over the top. But this shady little game had become irrelevant, as by that time, Trump's lead in the rest of the state was larger than the difference between the number of voters registered in Broward County and the number of ballots counted there. So I wrote, "It's over. Trump has won Florida." Knowing the electoral math was sealed, I went to bed, secure in the knowledge that Donald Trump had won the electoral vote, and with it, the presidency.

A little less than 12 hours later, at 9:31 AM, the Associated Press finally broke the bad news to SJWs around the world, "BREAKING: Donald Trump is elected president of the United States." Even to the very end, the media was reluctant to give up its Narrative and simply report the obvious truth to the American people. I knew, and all of my readers knew, that Trump's victory was inevitable, so how was it possible for the political experts and election analysts in the media to be unaware of the mathematical reality?

Regardless, Donald Trump won the presidential election and, in doing so, dealt such a crushing blow to the SJW Narrative that SJWs around the world are still reeling in complete disarray from the severity of their cognitive dissonance.

There are many useful lessons to be learned from the successful Trump campaign, and many books have been written about it and the man at the center of it. But as I am focused on SJWs, and better understanding and anticipating them, it is only the ways in which the successful Trump campaign exposed and illuminated SJW thinking and tactics that is of interest to us here. In this regard, consider how the Three Laws of SJW that were introduced in the preceding volume, *SJWs Always Lie*, could be readily observed in connection with the SJW opposition to President Trump, both before and after his inauguration.

First Law of SJW: SJWs Always Lie

> *"Trump and his minions are in the driver's seat, attempting to pose as respectable participants in American politics, when their views*

come out of a playbook written in German. *The playbook is Mein Kampf.*"

—Ron Rosenbaum, author of *Explaining Hitler: The Search for the Origins of His Evil*

"*The late U.S. Poet Laureate Dr. Maya Angelou once said, "When someone shows you who they are, believe them!" In other words, no one can hide his true nature. Never has this been more accurate for an American president than in the case of Donald Trump. Events in the aftermath of the violence in Charlottesville have made this abundantly clear. For the first time in our history, a Nazi sympathizer occupies the Oval Office.*"

—"Donald Trump Is a Nazi Sympathizer", *Foreign Policy*

"*Donald Trump the neo-Nazi sympathizer has achieved what Donald Trump the president has singularly failed to do: unite the nation.*"

—"The president of the United States is now a neo-Nazi sympathiser", *The Guardian*

"*Every day, and in countless and unexpected ways, Donald Trump, the President of the United States, finds new ways to divide and demoralize his country and undermine the national interest.*"

—"The Racial Demagoguery of Trump's Assaults on Colin Kaepernick and Steph Curry", *The New Yorker*

Second Law of SJW: SJWs Always Double Down

"I refuse to accept the US election results. We the first targets of Trump's xenophobic thuggery and dangerous delusions, we the Muslims, the Mexicans, the African-Americans, women, we are here at the forefront of defying Trump's ignominy. Along with millions of other Americans, we the most recent immigrants are now safely home at the dangerous delusions of an angry mob of white supremacist zombies shielding its wild fantasies behind democratic politics."

—Hamid Dabashi, Professor of Iranian Studies and
Comparative Literature at Columbia University

After Trump's victory (for which there were abundant signs in the preceding months), both the Democratic party and the big-city media urgently needed to do a scathingly honest self-analysis, because the election results plainly demonstrated that Trump was speaking to vital concerns (jobs, immigration, and terrorism among them) for which the Democrats had few concrete solutions.... Had Hillary won, everyone would have expected disappointed Trump voters to show a modicum of respect for the electoral results as well as for the historic ceremony of the inauguration, during which former combatants momentarily unite to pay homage to the peaceful transition of power in our democracy. But that was not the reaction of a vast cadre of Democrats shocked by Trump's win. In an abject failure of leadership that may be one of the most disgraceful episodes in the history of the modern Democratic party, Chuck Schumer, who had risen to become the Senate Democratic leader after the retirement of Harry Reid, asserted absolutely no moral authority as the party spun out of control in a nationwide orgy of rage and spite. Nor were there statesmanlike words of caution and restraint from two seasoned politicians whom I have admired for decades and believe should have run for president long ago—Senator Dianne Feinstein and Congresswoman Nancy Pelosi. How do Democrats imagine they can ever expand their electoral support if they go on and on in this self-destructive way, impugning half the nation as vile racists and homophobes?

—Camille Paglia, "On Trump, Democrats, Transgenderism, and Islamist Terror", *The Weekly Standard*

"What president?" Norman said late Sunday night by his locker after the team beat the Oakland Raiders 27-10. "Not my president.... I'm telling you right now, this man is not welcome in Washington, D.C. He's not. I hope he won't be around when I see him. He's not welcome. I can say that to your face. He's not welcome."

—"Redskins' Josh Norman: Donald Trump is 'not my president' ", *USA Today*

Third Law of SJW: SJWs Always Project

Hillary Clinton said Friday that Donald Trump is threatening America's democracy by not promising to accept the results of the presidential election. "We know, in our country, the difference between leadership and dictatorship. And the peaceful transition of power is something that sets us apart," Clinton told a crowd of about 1,600 at the Cuyahoga Community College in Cleveland.

—"Clinton: Trump 'threatens democracy' by not accepting election results", *Cincinnati Inquirer*

Hillary Clinton's campaign has refused to concede the election. Campaign chief John Podesta said that Ms Clinton won't be admitting defeat on election night.

—"Hillary Clinton refuses to concede election result
despite Donald Trump being on the edge of victory",
The Independent

In an interview Monday with NPR's Terry Gross, Clinton raised that critique up a notch—not only questioning the legitimacy of Trump's presidency but refusing to rule out the possibility of contesting the results if Russian collusion is proven by special counsel Bob Mueller.... This a big deal. The 2016 Democratic nominee, who won the popular vote by nearly 3 million votes, is expressly leaving open the possibility that she would pursue legal action to invalidate the last presidential election.

—"Hillary Clinton just floated the possibility of
contesting the 2016 election", *CNN Politics*,
28 September 2017

Nearly half of Republicans won't accept this election's results if the opposing candidate wins, according to a new Reuters-IPSOS poll. The survey, which was conducted online from Oct. 14 to Oct. 20, found that 49 percent of Republicans polled would not accept the legitimacy of this election if their candidate doesn't win. It also discovered that 67 percent of Republicans would perceive another candidate's victory as the result of illegal voting or election rigging.

—"Nearly half of Republicans won't accept the results if
Donald Trump loses", *Salon*, 25 October 2015

Since the election Tuesday night, we've had two days (and counting) of leftists literally taking to the streets to shout and cry and burn flags because their preferred candidate lost. More such protests are planned. In New York City, protesters chanted, "Not my president!" from the streets of midtown Manhattan around Trump's home on Fifth Avenue. In Oakland, Calif., rioters set garbage on fire, blocked traffic, attacked police and damaged local businesses.

—"The Left's hypocrisy on accepting election results",
Washington Examiner, 10 November 2016

Those are but a few examples of the Three Laws of Social Justice in action concerning the 2016 U.S. Presidential election and its fallout; it would have been tedious, but not terribly difficult, to provide several thousand more. Nor have Donald Trump's opponents calmed down much in the year following his election. Never-Trumpers, the moderate Republicans who supported every other Republican candidate during the primaries before turning to no-hoper Evan McMullin in the general election, hold firm in the faith that Trump is a puppet of Russia and Vladimir Putin, and regularly issue dire pronouncements about how Trump, his family members, and everyone who has associated with him are destined for prison. As was mentioned above, Team Clinton is still musing about the unlikely possibility of challenging the election results while more forward-thinking Democrats debate whether they should choose a black man, a black Muslim, or an Indian woman in 2020, or if they should simply go for broke and nominate an illegal alien.

The one thing we can be certain of is that Donald Trump will defeat whatever champion of social justice the Democrats put forward unless he fails to build America its promised big, beautiful wall.

Perhaps you may recall science fiction author John Scalzi, who provided the detailed example of the First Law of Social Justice in *SJWs Always Lie*. Here, in a post explaining his inability to write in 2017, he provides another useful example, this time of the psychological fragility of the SJWs and the way their defeat by traditional America at the moment of their expected triumph shook them to their core.

> *The thing is, the Trump era is a different kind of awful. It is, bluntly, unremitting awfulness. The man has been in office for nine months at this point and there is rarely a week or month where things have not been historically crappy, a feculent stew of Trump's s——— as a human and as a president, his epically corrupt and immoral administration, and the rise of worse elements of America finally feeling free to say, hey, in fact, they do hate Jews and gays and brown people. Maybe other people can focus when S—— America is large and in charge, but I'm finding it difficult to do.*

> *Here's one way to put it: Twelve years ago, when Hurricane Katrina hit and the US Government flubbed its response and hundreds died, I was so angry and upset that I almost vomited in sadness and anger. It's not an exaggeration, by the way—I literally felt like throwing up for a couple days straight. I eventually had to write "Being Poor" because it was either do that or go crazy. That was a week of feeling generally awful, and it wrecked me for another week after that. It took two weeks for me to get back on track with the novel I was writing at the time.*

> *Got it? Okay, listen: 2017 has been me feeling like I felt when Katrina hit every single f——— month of this year.*

—"2017, Word Counts and Writing Process", John Scalzi

Chapter 3

Defending the Narrative

"Social justice and social equality is every individual's responsibility to uphold and protect. Aside from the social justice issues that are recognized and not addressed, a whole slew of other social justice issues exist that have yet to be globally acknowledged."

—Pachamama Alliance

As I described in *SJWs Always Lie*, SJWs mindlessly following the social justice Narrative are rather like a school of fish, moving together in perfect harmony with every twist and turn it takes, no matter how convoluted or contradictory it might be. Each SJW is highly sensitive to the current position of the SJWs around him, which allows for rapid changes in direction according to the needs of the Narrative. George Orwell memorably labeled their thought processes in *1984*; the SJW ability to engage in doublethink permits them to readily accept that War is Peace, that day is night, that blacks cannot be racist, that kidnapping and torturing a white man is not a hate crime, that Russian intelligence denied Hillary Clinton the U.S. presidency, and every other momentary belief the Narrative requires them to simultaneously believe, no matter how absurd, or false, or self-contradictory it might be.

But occasionally, these sudden shifts prove too much for an SJW. Perhaps he is cursed with an unfortunate memory that recalls how yesterday, we were not at actually war with Eastasia, but Oceania. Or perhaps his mind is simply not flexible enough to accept the eighth impossible thing the *New York Times* requires him to believe before breakfast. In such cases, the SJW suddenly finds himself turning right while the rest of the school turns left and very quickly finds himself alone, defenseless, and much to his surprise, a high-priority target of his former friends.

Consider, for example, the surprise of gay, liberal journalist Glenn Greenwald, whose SJW credentials would seem to have been absolutely impeccable, when he observed there was no evidence that Russian President Vladimir Putin had engineered the electoral victory of Donald Trump in the U.S. presidential election, and that the idea that Putin might have done so was more than a little ridiculous.

I've done some, you know, pretty controversial and polarizing reporting in the past decade when I've been writing about politics. And when you do that, you obviously get attacked in lots of different ways. It's not just me; it's everybody who engages. It's just sort of the rough and tumble of politics and journalism. But I really haven't experienced anything even remotely like the smear campaign that has been launched by Democrats in this really coordinated way ever since I began just expressing skepticism about the prevailing narrative over Russia and its role that it allegedly played in the election and, in particular, in helping to defeat Hillary Clinton. I mean, not even the reporting I did based on the Edward Snowden archive, which was extremely controversial in multiple countries around the world, not even that compared to the attacks now.... But because Democrats are so desperate to put the blame on everybody but themselves for the complete collapse of their party, they're particularly furious at anybody who vocally challenges this narrative. And since I've been one of the people most vocally doing so, the smear campaign has been like none that I have ever encountered. I have been accused of being a member of the alt-right, of being an admirer of Breitbart, of being supportive of Donald Trump, of helping him get elected and, of course, of being a Kremlin operative. And it's just this constant flow, not from fringe accounts online, but from the Democratic operatives and pundits with the greatest influence. In fact, Howard Dean, the former chairman of the Democratic National Committee, went on Twitter three weeks ago and said, "I think it would be really interesting to find out whether The Intercept is receiving money from Russia or Iran"—something that he obviously has zero evidence or basis for suggesting, but this is what the Democratic Party has become.

—Glenn Greenwald, *Democracy Now*, 6 January 2017

It may have surprised Greenwald to have been accused of being on the payroll of Russia or Iran, but then, when one considers that Donald Trump, Donald Trump Jr., Michael Flynn, Michael Flynn Jr., Jared Kushner, Paul Manafort, Rex Tillerson, Jeff Sessions, Roger Stone, Carter Page, Michael Caputo, Michael Cohen, Nigel Farage, the *Fox & Friends* morning show, Mike Cernovich, Trey Gowdy, Valerie Plame Wilson, Adrien Chen, Julien Assange, and Wikileaks have all been similarly accused of being Kremlin spies, it was almost inevitable.

And given what we know of the Three Laws of Social Justice and the SJW tendency to project, it can hardly surprise the reader to learn that to date, the only actual evidence of Russian interference in the 2016 U.S. presidential election is $100,000 in Facebook ads bought between June 2015 and May 2017 on behalf of Hillary Clinton and the Democratic Party. The 3,000 ads "sought to sow discord among religious groups" and "highlighted support for Democrat Hillary Clinton among Muslim women."

The *Washington Post* headline: "Russian bought Facebook ads support Hillary Clinton, BLM". BLM, of course, refers to Black Lives Matter, the violent, rabble-rousing anti-police group that appears to be the primary cause of escalating homicide rates in cities such as Baltimore and Chicago. As a consequence of the BLM-inspired riots there, Baltimore had already seen more homicides by the middle of September 2017 than in all of 2002, when the television show *The Wire* was first broadcast and served as a showcase for the dangerous streets of the Maryland city.

Furthermore, according to Hillary Clinton's 2010 financial disclosure form, Renaissance Capital, a Russian investment bank, paid Bill Clinton $500,000 the same year that Hillary Clinton, as secretary of state, signed off on Russia's purchase of a controlling stake in Uranium One, a mining company with mines that produce more than 10 percent of the USA's total uranium production.

SJWs always project.

The fact that the social justice Narrative is reliably false is precisely the reason that SJWs defend it so ruthlessly. They know, as most of their opponents do not, that it will not stand up to detailed or prolonged scrutiny. That is why they react so harshly to even the most innocent questioning of it and why they respond as if they are being attacked when they are merely being questioned about it. Ironically, it is this oversensitive defensiveness of the Narrative that often leads neutral parties to begin having doubts about its truth, especially when they witness SJWs overreacting to those whose only crime is to have asked a few inconvenient questions.

The Narrative can be anything that SJWs believe to be in the interest of furthering social justice, large or small. It can be as big as the national anthem protests that have invited commentary from NFL owners and players to the league commissioner and President Trump, and it can be as small as a single image announcing the intention to crowdfund a new comic. In either case, the SJW response is almost invariably the same: to mischaracterize the nature of the dispute in a manner designed to discredit and disqualify the individual who has somehow caused the Narrative to be questioned.

Take the national anthem protests that have swept across the country and now have SJWs and other sympathizers taking a knee everywhere from concert stages and athletic fields to the floor of the

House of Representatives. Although they began as a protest of black oppression and lethal police brutality by former San Francisco 49ers quarterback Colin Kaepernick, a gesture punctuated by his decision to wear socks portraying policemen as pigs and a t-shirt celebrating a 1960 meeting of Malcolm X and Fidel Castro, they are now portrayed by SJWs as demonstrations of unity and opposition to President Trump. But there is no question that the protests, which have ranged from sitting or kneeling during the national anthem to refusing to take the field until after it has been played, are a demonstration of cultural war by blacks against the white American social order and its symbols. Colin Kaepernick explained as much to NFL Media in an interview after a preseason game between the 49ers and the Green Bay Packers on August 26, 2016.

"I am not going to stand up to show pride in a flag for a country that oppresses black people and people of color. To me, this is bigger than football and it would be selfish on my part to look the other way. There are bodies in the street and people getting paid leave and getting away with murder."

Since he opted out of his contract before being cut after the 2016 season, Kaepernick's protest probably would have been entirely forgotten by the time the 2017 season rolled around were it not for SJWs in the sports media creating a second false narrative. ESPN and other outlets such as ProFootballTalk spent most of the summer, and the entire preseason, complaining that the quarterback, who remained unsigned by all of the NFL's 32 teams, was only unable to find another job as a backup quarterback due to his willingness to speak out about his political views. The media pushed this second narrative hard all summer, claiming that Kaepernick was being blackballed even though his performance had observably declined since his appearance in Super Bowl XLVII in 2013. While it wasn't Kaepernick's fault that the 49ers finished 2-14 in 2016, second-worst in the league, the truth was that Kaepernick never really recovered from a disastrous

2015 season where he was injured, threw nearly as many intercep-
tions as touchdowns, and saw his QB rating drop from 98.3 in his
NFC Championship season to an abysmal 78.3, fifth-worst in the
league.

For the purposes of comparison, it is worth noting that there were
six quarterbacks with ratings over 100 that season. So, it was hardly
surprising that in a sport where the quarterback is the most important
player on the field by far, no quarterback-needy teams were willing to
sign a player who not only appeared to be in decline but was clearly
inclined to put himself and his political views ahead of the team and
its interests. Moreover, Kaepernick, like Tim Tebow and Robert
Griffin III, was more of an athlete than a proper quarterback and
required an offense designed to support his strengths and to conceal
his limitations, which no professional team will ever do for a backup
quarterback. Given that neither Tebow nor Griffin, both of whom
were also playoff quarterbacks in 2011 and 2013, respectively, are still
playing in the NFL, the media's narrative that Kaepernick was being
denied employment solely, or even primarily, due to his views simply
is not credible.

This did not prevent the SJW-converged sports media from foster-
ing the Kaepernick-as-martyr-for-free-speech narrative by publishing
gushing profiles with titles such as "Colin Kaepernick was the start
of what can be a better NFL", "We need more from white athletes
than gestures", "Aaron Rodgers believes Colin Kaepernick's protests
are the reason he's unsigned", and "The NFL can no longer hide from
the Colin Kaepernick movement."

But if the second narrative was unable to shame any NFL coaching
staff into signing the controversial player, it did suffice to inspire two
more players into action on Kaepernick's behalf. In Week One, five
players protested, including the three who had been protesting the
previous season, Michael Bennett of the Seahawks, Robert Quinn of
the Rams, and Eric Reid of the 49ers, who had been kneeling beside

Kaepernick from the start. The five players had a modicum of visible support from a handful of their teammates, particularly Reid, who was flanked by four of his standing teammates laying their hands on him.

The media did its best to build up public support for the protest, as *SB Nation* provided a roundup of all the protests throughout the league, complete with pictures, Mike Florio of *ProFootballTalk* complained that Kaepernick still did not have a job while Scott Tolzein, the second-string quarterback for the Indianapolis Colts, did. *Sports Illustrated* devoted an entire story to a reporter wearing a Kaepernick jersey to a game while *Fox Sports* gave anthem protester Michael Bennett a platform to lecture NFL fans about social justice on its Sunday pre-game show as well as helping him launch a podcast called *Head 2 Head.*

A few days later, the media was equally busy denying the possibility that all of this political activity in lieu of actual football had anything to do with the fact that the Week One television ratings declined from 12 to 28 percent. Even the fact that the worst decline was on the most conservative network, Fox, wasn't sufficient to convince them that defending the false narrative of Colin Kaepernick's victimhood was at least partially responsible for turning away viewers.

Enter Donald Trump. As a few more players, cheered on by the media, joined the initial protesters in Week Two, the President, never slow to sense when his opposition had planted its flag on shaky rhetorical ground, struck hard and fast with comments at a political rally in Alabama that shook the football world. "Wouldn't you love to see one of these NFL owners, when somebody disrespects our flag, to say, 'Get that son of a bitch off the field right now. Out! He's fired. He's fired!' You know, some owner is going to do that. He's going to say, 'That guy that disrespects our flag, he's fired.' And that owner, they don't know it, they'll be the most popular person in this country."

As the President no doubt anticipated, the media and the players immediately doubled down. As the media uniformly shrieked in outrage and denounced Trump's comments as unpresidential, the players sported black shirts with #IMWITHKAP on them in their pre-game warmups, 180 players kneeled during the national anthem, three whole teams (less one Steelers tackle) remained in their locker rooms until after the anthem was over, and two-thirds of the owners issued statements that either condemned the President or expressed support for the players' protest, which was now increasingly directed at the President as well as the anthem and the flag. The NFL even ignored its own game operations manual in favor of releasing a mealy-mouthed statement condemning the President's comments for being divisive.

The National Anthem must be played prior to every NFL game, and all players must be on the sideline for the National Anthem. During the National Anthem, players on the field and bench area should stand at attention, face the flag, hold helmets in their left hand, and refrain from talking. The home team should ensure that the American flag is in good condition. It should be pointed out to players and coaches that we continue to be judged by the public in this area of respect for the flag and our country. Failure to be on the field by the start of the National Anthem may result in discipline, such as fines, suspensions, and/or the forfeiture of draft choice(s) for violations of the above, including first offenses.

—*NFL Game Operations Manual*, NFL Game Operations
Department

In a beautiful example of defending the Narrative through sophistry and deception, the media rushed to debunk reports that emerged on social media claiming the NFL rules required the players to be on the field and stand for the anthem because, as it turned out, it was actually just the NFL policies laid out in the operations manual instead of the rulebook. Either way, the NFL promptly declared that regardless of whether it was a rule or a policy that had been so publicly violated, the NFL had no intention of disciplining anyone for disrespecting the flag, the anthem, the military, the veterans, the fallen, the nation, and the President, and on a day that had been decreed Gold Star Mother's Day in 1936. The NFL's halfhearted appeal to free expression might have been more convincing had it not prevented the Dallas Cowboys from honoring five Dallas police officers murdered at a Black Lives Matter protest in 2016, and threatened to fine six players who wore cleats on September 11 in remembrance of the victims of the terror attacks 16 years before. As it was, literally no one even pretended to buy it, despite heroic efforts on the part of the media SJWs to sell the NFL and its commissioner, Roger Goodell, as unlikely champions of free speech.

It was no surprise to me, or anyone else who paid attention to Trump's electoral campaign, to observe that the President had clearly anticipated the firestorm of criticism he provoked. Indeed, I believe he was expecting the media, the players, and the league to aggressively double down in the way that they did because, as I witnessed in the case of the Rabid Puppies and the Hugo Award, the immediate reaction of SJWs called out in public is to cry foul, to summon reinforcements, and to try to intimidate the opposition by a public show of apparent mass support. And while the response by the players, the media, and the NFL was impressive, it was overwhelmed by the massive demonstration of disapproval by NFL spectators, who are not only disproportionately made up of Trump voters but are arguably the most patriotic, flag-waving Americans this side of NASCAR. The NFL's rhetoric about unity, racial harmony, and free expression was about as effective as the defense of the winless 2008 Detroit Lions, as an explosion of outrage among NFL fans led to a rapid drop in game attendance, television viewers, approval ratings, and merchandise sales.

Consider the immediate short-term consequences:

- NBC's "Sunday Night Football" down 15 percent.

- Fox's Sunday afternoon game down 19 percent.

- 34 percent of Americans say they are less likely to watch an NFL game.

- President Trump's approval ratings rose.

- The Ravens stadium immediately erupted in boos when the team kneeled before the national anthem.

- "Atlanta, 10 minutes into 3rd quarter in a 14–10 game. Most seats empty."

- "The Green Bay Packers and Pittsburgh Steelers, in particular, each had received significant blowback from their fan bases and sponsors."

In other words, this was an absolutely devastating trap set for the SJWs in the media and the league office by an expert rhetorician who knew that SJWs are always predisposed to aggressively defend their Narrative. It was rather like watching an army allowed to dangerously extend itself on a strategic map, then hit hard in the flank, cut off, and surrounded by a brilliant enemy general. The entire episode was a veritable master class in rhetorical strategy. By the next week, the number of protesting players had fallen dramatically, the National Basketball Association announced that any attempt to protest the national anthem would be met with discipline from the league office, and it only appears to be a matter of time before the NFL itself is going to be forced to publicly retreat from its unpopular position.

At least one member of the sports media, Jason Whitlock, understood how the President played the media, the NFL, and the players perfectly due to his ability to predict their actions. On the MMQB podcast with Peter King, Whitlock said, "He baited us, and they fell for it unbelievably. Oh my god, he says we shouldn't kneel, so let's everybody kneel together. Let's show Donald Trump! These guys are involved in a business where they make millions of dollars, and Trump just baited them into being adversarial with their customer base."

One of the most remarkable things about the determination, or rather, the psychological need, of SJWs to defend their Narrative at all costs is the way in which they will do so without hesitation even as the Narrative itself mutates in real time. I witnessed literally hundreds of examples of this personally when in late September 2017, the publishing house for which I am the Lead Editor, Castalia House, announced a crowdfunding campaign for its new graphic novel series called Alt★Hero. I created the series in response to many requests from comics fans who were in despair at the complete convergence of the comics industry, which is addressed later in this book. The plan was to foxnews Marvel, DC, Image, Dark Horse, and the various lesser players in the industry just like Roger Ailes did when he founded Fox News and rapidly became the top news channel due to having 50 percent of the American TV-viewing public to himself while ABC, CNN, NBC, CBS, MSNBC, and PBS all battled among themselves for the other 50 percent.

The difference is that Marvel, the industry leader, has pulled the comics industry so far to the Left as a result of a complete takeover by SJWs that their various series no longer hold any appeal to about three-quarters of the potential comics-reading audience. As always, the challenge is in the execution, but there can be no denying that the opportunity is an incredible one.

And somewhat to my surprise, I discovered the SJWs in the industry even appear to be dimly aware of their extreme vulnerability now. But that didn't prevent them from defending the Narrative and doing what SJWs always do—lie, double down, and project—when they became aware of the unlikely challenge being posed to their dominance of the comics industry.

Unlike video games and science fiction, SJWs consider the comics to have been their turf from the start. They particularly revere Jack Kirby, an influential artist who worked closely with Stan Lee at Marvel and helped create some of the most famous superheroes and supervillains, including the Fantastic Four, the Avengers, the Hulk, Thor, Iron Man, the original X-Men, Doctor Doom, Magneto, and the Black Panther. They regard Kirby, a World War II veteran with a penchant for unlikely tall tales, as a proto-SJW; science-fiction SJW turned Marvel writer Saladin Ahmed even described Kirby as "the original comic book social justice warrior" and praised him for being the first comic book artist to draw black and Asian characters.

I didn't know much about comics, but due to the success of Castalia House in both fiction and nonfiction, I'd been hearing more and more from comic book fans in despair over the increasing convergence of the industry and the way in which their favorite characters were being disappeared and replaced by perverse SJW versions. So, in April 2017, I announced that Castalia House was working on a new comic which I named Alt-Hero, to reflect the fact that the heroic values of the past were now deemed an alternative by the converged mainstream. I also mentioned that while we planned to crowdfund the comic, we would not be using Kickstarter, due to the probability that Kickstarter would respond to complaints by SJWs by shutting down the campaign.

This announcement was greeted with promises of support by my readership and was almost entirely ignored by everyone else. But one SJW trolling the blog provided a highly accurate preview of the eventual reaction by the social justice masses when he declared, "You are afraid of KS because you know that you can't earn much money there and that your lack of popular support would then be revealed. That is why they don't fear you, there is nothing to fear. You trying to run a KS campaign would be your defeat."

I figured that receiving a response clearly intended to demoralize and dissuade me only one hour and 56 minutes after posting the announcement was an excellent sign that we were over the target and mentioned as much on my blog. But that was pretty much it for the next five months, as the artists and I prepared for the campaign while waiting for Freestartr, the free-speech friendly crowdfunding site, to come online. While we considered using Indie-Go-Go, which has proven less amenable to SJW pressure, the chance to support a genuine Alt-Tech site struck me as being the wiser option, even though I knew that the new platform would mean a considerably less visible crowdfunding campaign for us.

Fortunately, we had the SJW need to Defend the Narrative working in our favor. Only days before the launch, I finally got back to an artist who was interested in working on what was now named Alt★Hero, and signed him to provide the art for our third book. I had him revise the artwork for a character I'd created called Rebel, who was a freckled, auburn-haired Southron belle wearing a Confederate flag top with a white-starred blue mask. I liked his take on her so much so that we worked her into the launch video on the final revision and created a simple graphic with Rebel, the Alt★Hero logo, and the words "COMING SOON" on a red background.

Now, I knew the image would trigger the SJWs on social media. Their counterparts in the comics industry have been working hard in recent years to make female figures less attractive, methodically chopping off their hair, thickening their waists, reducing the size of their breasts, and, in some cases, turning them into sexually ambiguous figures that resemble men. So, a hot chick with long hair wearing a push-up bustier was always going to set them off, particularly one who was also wearing Daisy Dukes and cowboy boots.

But it was the Confederate flag that was like waving a red flag in front of a particularly short-tempered bull. Coming only a few months after the Charlottesville protests in which the media whipped up the less educated SJWs into an anti-historical frenzy that had them beheading and defacing statues of everyone from Robert E. Lee and Stonewall Jackson to Abraham Lincoln, Christopher Columbus, and, for some reason, the mayor of Philadelphia from 1972 to 1980,

Frank Rizzo, the idea that the Confederate flag could be worn by a superheroine in the current year turned out to be massively triggering. The image sparked literally thousands of tweets, three-quarters of them from furious SJWs, and for an as-yet-nonexistent comic, the engagement was off the charts, with 191,149 impressions, 59,806 engagements, and an engagement rate of 31.3 percent, which was 11.6 times higher than my average rate.

This over-the-top outrage even inspired me to paraphrase Gandhi in creating the SJW REEEEEE sequence, "REEEEEE" referring to the sound SJWs metaphorically make when they are triggered. It turned out to be a very reliable predictor of the average SJWs reaction to Alt★Hero, although more than a few SJWs were so triggered that they couldn't even manage to pretend to be indifferent and skipped step two.

1. First they "laugh". So hard.

2. Then they don't care. At all.

3. Then they get mad. REALLY, REALLY MAD!

4. And then they go silent.

It really was rather remarkable how indistinguishable the various reactions were, and how closely they tended to follow the sequence over time. Virtually every SJW initially began by "lol," "lmao," "lmfao," "hahahahahaha," "HAHAHAHAHAHA," or some other variation on this theme. But rather than responding to their fake laughter, I ignored it and increased the pressure by focusing on another trigger point, namely, their reverence for Jack Kirby.

Now, you have to understand that I really had no idea who Jack Kirby was, other than a vague impression that he had worked with Marvel's Stan Lee at one point in time. But his name was invoked frequently by the SJWs when they weren't laughing too hard to do so, and so I pointed out that these days, the SJWs who run Marvel and DC would consider him problematic, and so he would prefer to work with me. As it turns out, this was almost certainly wrong because I subsequently learned that Kirby was a very small man who portrayed himself as a streetfighter and was a teller of tall tales about both his World War II experiences and his pre-war habit of punching Nazis. In other words, he really was a proto-SJW, and were he alive today, would probably be advocating transgender Iron Man and gay Muslim Captain America as fervently as anyone else in the industry.

This somehow led to the bizarre response of SJWs repeatedly threatening me with being beaten up by the corpse of Jack Kirby. Lest you think I am inventing this, here are but a few examples.

- *You don't know a f——— thing about Jack Kirby, do you? If he were alive he'd beat your ass for not keeping his name out your damn mouth.*

- *Jack Kirby would have literally beat you to death even in his later years.*

- *Jack Kirby would beat you to death with his bare hands.*

- *Kirby would beat the hell out of you, friend.*

- *jack kirby would of wooped your ass and then tell the story for laughs at parties for years*

- *If Jack Kirby were alive today he'd beat the living s—— out of you without hesitation and burn you a good one with his cigar to boot.*

- *"The only real politics I knew was that if a guy liked Hitler, I'd beat the stuffing out of him and that would be it." —Jack Kirby, 1990*

Now, you would have to see pictures of Jack Kirby and me to understand how these utterly ridiculous responses are even funnier than they sound. Kirby was a midget about 5'3" tall and he might have weighed 120 pounds dripping wet. Alive or dead, he wasn't going to beat up any grown man, let alone one who dwarfed him like Thor towering over the teenage Spider-Man. SJWs can be seriously weird.

But however weird their triggered responses, I was encouraged by them because they were spreading the word about Alt★Hero far wider than I could have ever accomplished on my own. Knowing this, I poured more gasoline on the fire by questioning Kirby's artistic talent, pointing out his tendency to draw hands with excessively long little fingers, noting his habit of drawing women without necks, and observing the improbability of some of his more exaggerated war stories.

As you might expect, the SJWs reacted to these provocations in the calm and measured way for which they are so justly known. Their sacred Narrative of the great Jack Kirby was not merely being questioned, but it was being publicly violated, and the resulting REEEEEEs may well have alerted alien races many light-years away of the fact of our existence.

The end result of this mass triggering of SJWs was more than satisfactory. Late in the evening on September 28, 2017, Castalia House launched the Alt★Hero campaign on Freestartr, hoping to raise $25,000 in 30 days. I posted an announcement on Vox Popoli, did a short Periscope to announce it, and went to bed. By the time I woke up, the campaign was fully funded, having hit the initial funding goal in only four hours. It closed out the end of the first day at $37,000, and as of the time of this writing, had reached its first six stretch goals, with 1,077 backers contributing more than $97,000 to produce nine volumes of the new comic.

The lesson is this: while defying the SJW Narrative and fighting back in the cultural war is absolutely necessary for the survival of Western civilization, the predictability of the thought police can be also exploited for fun, political leverage, and even profit.

Chapter 4

Convergence and the Corporation

"Society should treat all equally well who have deserved equally well of it, that is, who have deserved equally well absolutely. This is the highest abstract standard of social and distributive justice; towards which all institutions, and the efforts of all virtuous citizens should be made in the utmost degree to converge."

—John Stuart Mill, *Utilitarianism*, 1861

Convergence is the ultimate destination for all organizations infiltrated by SJWs and all individuals who devote themselves to the philosophy of social justice. For an organization, convergence is the process of transforming all of its existing priorities and purposes and redirecting them towards those that serve the interests of social justice while for an individual, convergence is the transformation of his beliefs and opinions, and even his appearance, to conform to the current social justice Narrative.

Any kind of organization can be converged. Every type of organization has been converged. From churches to science fiction conventions, from rock bands to research science fellowships, there is not a single organization that has demonstrated itself to be immune to SJW convergence. Even ancient organizations, such as the Roman Catholic Church, have shown themselves to be susceptible to SJW infiltration, corruption, and convergence. And, remarkably enough, we have even seen that as the adherents of social justice gain more power and influence throughout the West, they have developed the ability to forcibly converge organizations from the outside. They no longer even need to obtain entry to an organization or an institution to converge it but instead can simply exert social and financial pressure in order to force it to transform its operations and objectives.

Convergence is, in some ways, like a societal cancer. Once an individual is successfully converged and accepts the social justice Narrative in place of his previous religion, politics, and philosophy, that individual will usually begin to proselytize for one form of SJW Narrative or another and will either attempt to corrupt other individuals he encounters or begin to start trying to converge the organizations to which he belongs. The more fully that an organization is converged, the harder it is for the non-SJW to survive in that organization, and the more organizations that are converged, the easier it is to impose social justice principles and practices on other organizations as well as individuals outside those organizations.

Remember, Mill stated that all institutions and all virtuous citizens "should be made" to converge. Unlike Christianity or even Islam, social justice does not present one with a choice to accept it or not. The only question is whether the SJW possesses sufficient power and influence to force your submission or not.

And thanks to the increasing convergence of corporate America, particularly the Fortune 500, that power and influence has steadily grown over the past three decades. The technology leaders, particularly the social media giants, have not only rejected the patriotic GM model famously articulated by the former U.S. Secretary of Defense and CEO of General Motors, "what was good for our country was good for General Motors, and vice versa," but have turned it completely on its head. Now patriotism is divisiveness, and the most important corporate priority is no longer maximizing shareholder value or customer satisfaction, but demonstrating superior global citizenship through corporate dedication to tolerance, equality, progress, inclusiveness, and diversity. Instead of market or technological leadership, this new breed of SJW CEOs now seek to provide moral leadership to a world that neither hired them nor asked for it.

Apple's Tim Cook, who succeeded legendary founder Steve Jobs as the landmark computer manufacturer's CEO, is a prime example of the new breed of technology executive. Smart, well-educated, progressive, and typically possessing one or more Diversity attributes, these SJW technology executives are given to delivering pious corporate lectures as full of social justice platitudes as technological jargon. They see their influential positions as more than just very highly-paid jobs, but as platforms for effecting the social change they deem desirable.

> *Mr. Cook is one of the many business leaders in the country who appear to be filling the void, using his platform at Apple to wade into larger social issues that typically fell beyond the mandate of executives in past generations. He said he had never set out to do so, but he feels he has been thrust into the role as virtually every large American company has had to stake out a domestic policy.... Watching Mr. Cook over the years, I've been fascinated to see how he has become as animated when talking about big issues like education and climate change as he is when talking about Apple.*
>
> —"Apple's Tim Cook Barnstorms for 'Moral Responsibility' ", Andrew Ross Sorkin, *The New York Times*

Although notorious for their commitment to various social justice fads, Apple is far from the most-converged technology giant. Intel has launched a $300 million Global Diversity and Inclusion initiative that has adopted as a slogan the rather dubious phrase "innovation begins with inclusion." This is not only a strange motto for a company founded by two straight white men, Gordon Moore and Robert

Noyce, but flies directly in the face of the entire history of Western science and technological innovation. Twitter, which is considerably less innovative, but every bit as committed to social justice as Intel, established its Orwellian-sounding Trust and Safety Council in co-operation with rabid SJW-infested organizations such as the Anti-Defamation League, GLAAD, Hollaback, the Wahid Foundation, and something called Jugendschutz. One can only presume that the Hitler Youth were otherwise occupied, or they would have been invited, too.

The idea behind the Trust and Safety Council is that people who are being bullied and otherwise tormented by bad people, as defined by the SJWs on the Council, will have their accounts temporarily frozen and shadowbanned while links to websites deemed fraudulent, dangerous, or otherwise undesirable will be blocked, and the most egregious offenders will be summarily banned from Twitter.

Being a Grade A crimethinker and confirmed Narrative denier, I have, of course, been subject to most of the Trust and Safety Council's disciplinary actions. I was locked out of my account for several months for the crime of linking to my own blog, have been regularly shadowbanned, and was sentenced to Twitter jail for one week after responding to an aggressive SJW who had been attacking me with a meme. Twitter jail is rather interesting, as one is still allowed to access Twitter but cannot tweet, retweet, or like anyone else's tweets. The clever thing is that while Twitter still permits the jailbird to click on the various functions, doing so not only does not work, but automatically adds three hours to your sentence without informing you that it has done so. As an Award-Winning Cruelty Artist, I can only applaud this petty sadism, but as a game designer, I have to question the probable effect on long-term customer satisfaction.

And while I've never been banned from Twitter, as Milo Yiannopou-los was for offending Saturday Night Live actress Leslie Jones, for more than a year, any attempt to link to my blog is met with the following message.

This request looks like it might be automated. To protect our users from spam and other malicious activity, we can't complete this action right now. Please try again later.

As they say, SJWs always lie. But what I find most interesting about all of these thought policing efforts is their utter futility. This is something that we can measure very easily, thanks to Twitter Analytics. When I was first locked out of my account in September 2016, I had 20k followers and was getting 6.5 million impressions per month. After nearly one year of periodic interference with my account, as of the end of August 2017, I had 33k followers and registered 14.5 million impressions that month. Twitter may have managed to slow the growth of my Twitter account; I am well behind both Mike Cernovich's 335k followers and Jack Posobiec's 193k followers, just to name two fellow Castalia House authors who are not exactly beloved by SJWs. But if the best efforts of the Trust and Safety Council have only managed to slow a notorious thought criminal to 65 percent and 123 percent annual growth, we can safely conclude that those efforts are doomed to failure.

What the council has managed to bring about, however, is Peak Twitter. Twitter's seemingly inexorable growth slammed to a halt in the first quarter of 2017 and then declined by two million users in the second quarter. While this is a drop in the bucket considering that it amounts to only a 2.9 percent reduction in the number of users, this demonstrates, once more, the truth of the Impossibility of Social Justice Convergence. Twitter's business mandate is to grow, but the social justice mandate of its Trust and Safety Council is to expel and punish Twitter's disfavored users.

But far and away the most egregious social justice warrior among the new breed of technology CEOs is Mark Zuckerberg.

For the past decade, Facebook has focused on connecting friends and families. With that foundation, our next focus will be developing the social infrastructure for community—for supporting us, for keeping us safe, for informing us, for civic engagement, and for inclusion of all.

Bringing us all together as a global community is a project bigger than any one organization or company, but Facebook can help contribute to answering these five important questions:

How do we help people build supportive communities that strengthen traditional institutions in a world where membership in these institutions is declining?

How do we help people build a safe community that prevents harm, helps during crises and rebuilds afterwards in a world where anyone across the world can affect us?

How do we help people build an informed community that exposes us to new ideas and builds common understanding in a world where every person has a voice?

How do we help people build a civically-engaged community in a world where participation in voting sometimes includes less than half our population?

How do we help people build an inclusive community that reflects our collective values and common humanity from local to global levels, spanning cultures, nations and regions in a world with few examples of global communities?

My hope is that more of us will commit our energy to building the long term social infrastructure to bring humanity together. The answers to these questions won't all come from Facebook, but I believe we can play a role.

Our job at Facebook is to help people make the greatest positive impact while mitigating areas where technology and social media can contribute to divisiveness and isolation. Facebook is a work in progress, and we are dedicated to learning and improving. We take our responsibility seriously, and today I want to talk about how we plan to do our part to build this global community.

—Building Global Community, Mark Zuckerberg,
17 February 2017

Due to its excellent infrastructure and talented programmers, Facebook has built the closest thing to a corporate panopticon in human history. Its only real limits have been imposed by national governments that don't trust Facebook encroaching on what they consider to be their domain of state surveillance. And while Facebook has attempted to accommodate the interests of its state competitors, as evidenced by Zuckerberg's personal alliance with German Reichskanzler Angela Merkel and his failed attempts to curry favor with China— at one Obama administration state dinner, the ever-autistic Zuckerberg actually asked Chinese president Xi Jinping to name his unborn daughter; Xi politely declined—its global ambitions will tend to be curtailed over time by the inevitable fragmentation of the Internet into national internets.

Nevertheless, Facebook remains one of the greatest threats to individual privacy and freedom in human history, particularly because it is headed by a sincere and committed social justice warrior. The global community Mark Zuckerberg is attempting to build is one that is fully converged, totally dedicated to social justice, has no respect for the Christian traditions of the West, and is intrinsically opposed to the historical values of America's Founding Fathers. It is a danger to everyone on the planet, even those who erroneously believe themselves to be protected by their fame, their money, or their power.

The Weaponized Corporation

Many individuals have believed, incorrectly, that they were immune
to the enmity of social justice warriors. Consider the examples of two
very different individuals who were vastly more successful, independent, and antifragile than the average individual, Milo Yiannopoulos
and Felix Kjellberg, both of whom were to discover that neither
success nor independence is necessarily a sufficient defense against a
concerted SJW attack.

At the beginning of 2017, Milo Yiannopolous was a rising star
in political and media circles. He had completed an extraordinarily
successful tour of U.S. college campuses, his book *Dangerous* was a
#1 bestseller on Amazon prior to its upcoming release by Simon &
Schuster, and he was employed as the Tech Editor of Breitbart News,
an organization that was considered to be well to the right of Fox
News, and therefore, seemingly impervious to any amount of SJW
pressure. Not only that, but Milo had very nearly reached single-
name status as an outrageous political provocateur, as his quick wit,
flamboyant charm, and unrepentant homosexuality rendered him all
but impervious to a very hostile media. In Britain, he ran rings around
his would-be discreditors, invariably leaving them wide eyed with
shock and slack jawed with horror as he won over live audiences and
television audiences alike with seemingly effortless ease. At Berkeley,
his appearance sparked a massive Antifa riot that caused millions of
dollars of damage and set the stage for the public discourse on free
speech for the next six months.

The media desperately attempted to tar him as a racist, as a Nazi, as
a white supremacist, as the leader of GamerGate, as the leader of the
Alt-Right, as a fraud, as a con artist, an antisemite, and pretty much
every other disqualifying label they could manage to spell. But it
wasn't until an appearance on Bill Maher's HBO show combined with
an invitation to speak at the Conservative Political Action Conference
demonstrated the real risk of the British provocateur breaking through

into the American mainstream that opposition research unearthed a few ill-considered remarks he had made in an interview with Joe Rogan two years before that they finally managed to find a rhetorical weapon capable of landing effective shots on him. More importantly, they were able to reach the corporations through which he derived his income.

Accustomed to evading rhetorical blasts rather than absorbing them, and to ducking punches rather than evading them, Milo found it impossible to respond to the malicious and defamatory accusations of him endorsing and defending pedophilia with his usual aplomb. A victim of teenage molestation and outspoken critic of genuine pedophile defenders at Salon and on social media, he went uncharacteristically dark for a few days before emerging to give an interview in which he appeared to be genuinely shaken. Sensing an opportunity, SJWs immediately swarmed. Simon & Schuster canceled his book contract despite it being a #1 Amazon bestseller; a few days later, Breitbart cut its ties with him.

Felix Kjellberg was an even more unlikely, and seemingly less vulnerable target. The most popular YouTube sensation on the planet, PewDiePie, as he is more commonly known, had 53 million subscribers on YouTube and his own network on MakerStudios where he played video games and presented silly montages. However, MakerStudios was bought by Disney in 2014, and after the *Wall Street Journal* publicized the fact that nine of PewDiePie's hundreds of videos contained momentary clips of anti-semitic or Nazi-related images. Despite the fact that the video clips were obviously satirical and in no way serious—one was a group of Sri Lankan men holding up a sign that read "Death to All Jews" while another featured Jesus saying "Hitler did absolutely nothing wrong"—Disney cut its ties with Kjellberg and denounced him for being "inappropriate" and clearly being too "provocative and irreverent."

YouTube reacted as well, although more moderately, as it demonetized one third of his videos, canceled the second season of

Scare PewDiePie, and removed the PewDiePie channel from Google Preferred. Kjellberg, suitably chastened, vowed to be more family friendly, promising, "No more swearing, no more sexual jokes, and definitely no more Hitler jokes. I wish I was joking. I'm not. It seems that YouTube has made some changes, and about a third of my videos have become demonetized. I'm going to have to be family friendly from now on so I don't go homeless. I love money too much."

As he remains on YouTube and now has 57 million subscribers, Kjellberg appears to be safe for the moment, but as has already been demonstrated to him, his entire platform can be taken away should he again behave in a manner deemed excessively inappropriate or too provocative by SJWs at his corporate master.

That particular corporate master, Google, demonstrated the limits of its tolerance very publicly in August 2017, when a 10-page internal document titled "Google's Ideological Echo Chamber" that criticized the company's heavily SJW diversity culture was leaked to the public. The author of what was subsequently described as a viewpoint diversity manifesto, James Damore, was fired, and in a statement remarkable for its textbook SJW doubletalk, Google CEO Sundar Pichai claimed the firing was due to Damore's memo violating Google's Code of Conduct by advancing harmful gender stereotypes in the workplace.

A surprising number of Google employees were angered by Pichai's action, nearly a third of them indicated in an internal poll that they did not approve of it, and several of them with whom I am connected sent me a series of screencaps from Google's internal communications system that painted an ugly picture of how completely out of control many of Google's SJW employees had become. I posted a few of excerpts from them on Vox Popoli, and tweeted several memes that paired direct quotes with pictures of the SJWs responsible. These excerpts and tweets were picked up by Breitbart Tech as well as other sites and spread rapidly around the Internet; needless to say, it didn't take long to get back to the people at Google.

To see the full extent of the SJW convergence at Google was pretty astonishing, even though I had been told about it months before by multiple Googlers, as they call themselves. Google had always been that way, but things had gotten increasingly out of hand ever since the election of Donald Trump had apparently unhinged more than a few of them. I did not post most of the screencaps I received, so this is the first time some of the following comments by Google managers and directors have been seen by outsiders. When reading them, keep in mind that these Google employees felt perfectly comfortable making these comments about their colleagues openly in Google's internal corporate communication system. To the best of my knowledge, none of them ended up meeting the same fate as James Damore.

- *There are certain alternative views, including different political views, which I do not want people to share here. My tolerance ends at my friends' terror. You can believe that women or minorities are unqualified all you like—I can't stop you—but if you say it out loud, then you deserve what's coming to you. Yes, this is "silencing". I intend to silence these views; they are violently offensive.... I'm fine with conservatives, but they must actually have human souls.*

- *Will the author ever be promoted again? If the author is promoted, we send a clear signal that their work output—the work output of a single engineer—is worth more than the irreparable harm their document has caused to 1000s of Googlers. If the author is promoted, we grant him more power and influence to harm Googlers that don't fit his bigoted worldview.... There is no reason for the author to remain here and only damage can come of it.*

- *God, please let our inevitable public statement be less toothless than that internal mail. We need to say "Wow, that was some bullshit right there. We've fired that guy into the sun and updated our code of conduct to say not to do anything that looks even a bit like that, ever. Also, we're looking at how we can change our interview processes to notice toxic opinions like that, because seriously, wtf, where did that come from?*

- *So, let me be straight. These are shitty opinions. I say this with all my hats on; ally, director, manager, human. They are the antithesis of what we're trying to do at Google; they are intellectually lazy, biased, and unkind. They have no place here.... Leave it at home. IF you're not prepared to live it at home, then leave yourself there.*

- *Google HR—don't be mean to actual Nazis they are valued coworkers. Me:: They're Nazis. No. I will absolutely go out of my way to make sure I never work near anyone involved with or who endorsed that garbage. Because Nazis. And you should absolutely punch Nazis.*

- *From now on, I'm going to devote at least the first third of my 45 minute interview time to a discussion of experience with diversity. If the first fifteen minutes doesn't satisfy me, I'll continue the discussion. If need be, it will take forty-five minutes. I would encourage others to do the same.*

- *While Google appears to be doing very little to quell the hostile voices that exist inside the company, I want those hostile voices to know: I will never, ever hire/transfer you onto my team. Ever. I don't care if you are a perfect fit, or technically excellent or whatever. I will actively not work with you, even to the point where your team or product is impacted by this decision. I'll communicate why to your manager if it comes up. You're being blacklisted by people at companies outside of Google. You might not have been aware of this, but people know, people talk. There are always social consequences.*

- *One of the great things about Google's internal communication mechanisms (G+, mailing lists, etc), is that, as a manager, I can easily go find out if I really want to work with you.... I keep a written blacklist of people whom I will never allow on or near my team, based on how they view and treat their coworkers. That blacklist got a little longer today.*

These Google SJWs did not react at all well to discovering that their tantrums were not merely being broadcast to the entire company, where they knew they would be safely ignored, but to the entire world, where they were not. Internal alarms went off, more name-calling ensued, dire predictions were made, and the entire company promptly went into lockdown mode.

Google CEO Sundar Pichai has canceled the company's much-anticipated meeting to talk about gender issues today. The move came after some of its employees expressed concern over online harassment they had begun to receive after their questions and names have been published outside the company on a variety of largely alt-right sites.

"We had hoped to have a frank, open discussion today as we always do to bring us together and move forward. But our Dory questions appeared externally this afternoon, and on some websites Googlers are now being named personally," wrote Pichai to employees. "Googlers are writing in, concerned about their safety and worried they may be 'outed' publicly for asking a question in the Town Hall."

Pichai was set to address the search giant's 60,000 employees in 30 minutes in an all-hands meeting about a recent post by recently fired employee James Damore. In it, the software engineer claimed that women might not be as good as men at tech because of biological reasons, like "neuroticism." In other words, they could not handle stress and high pressure as much…. Several sites like this one [this was literally a link to my blog —VD] have been publishing internal discussion posts and giving out information on those employees.

In addition, in a move that many Googlers found already disturb-ing, Damore did his first major interview with alt-right YouTube personality, Stefan Molyneux (ironic, I know, since Google owns the online video giant).

—"Google CEO Sundar Pichai canceled an all-hands
meeting about gender controversy due to employee
worries of online harassment", *Recode*, 10 August 2017

By "online harassment," the employees actually meant "people finding out that we were threatening and harassing our colleagues." But you knew that, of course, because SJWs always project. And given that SJWs always double down, the fact that Google did not pull the plug on my Blogger blog and my Gmail account as I half-expected tends to indicate that there are still some sane elements reining in the social justice warriors in the interest of actually pursuing conventional business objectives, as did their relatively restrained response to the PewDiePie affair. That being said, it is probably only a matter of time before the growing mass of SJWs within Google manage to converge the company entirely, at which point it is likely to go the way of Facebook and officially make social justice its primary corporate objective.

What is perhaps most remarkable, however, and demonstrates that literally no one on the planet is entirely safe from potential SJW swarming and personal destruction, is the unexpected fate of the gender-confused queer rock band PWR BTTM. A mildly punkish two-piece drum-and-guitar band with a penchant for simple riffs and catchy melodies, they write short songs with titles like "Ugly Cherries," "I Wanna Boi," and "Dairy Queen," and are vaguely rem-iniscent of a more restrained Electric Six. They consider themselves to be advocates for gay pride and queer visibility and make a regular habit of wearing more makeup than Adam Ant, David Bowie, and Prince combined. They also prefer to use gender-neutral honorifics, switch instrument roles in the middle of their concert sets, and refer to themselves as Mx. Bruce and Mx. Hopkins.

It is more difficult to imagine a more SJW-approved rock band than this pair of musical performance artistes. And indeed, they were the darlings of the college tour circuit until a photo appeared of Hopkins standing on a beach five years before, next to a swastika drawn in the sand. Hopkins made the elementary mistake of apologizing for his past insensitivity, explained that it was merely "a time in my life where I thought being 'politically incorrect' was really funny and had literally no concept of my actions," and assured everyone that the photo did not represent who he is today.

Unsurprisingly, his (or her, or xir, or whatever pronoun Hopkins happens to use these days) apology went over about as well as past apologies from Nobel Prize-winning scientists have, and SJWs promptly swarmed the band. Accusations of sexual misconduct and "boundary-crossing behavior" were made, and despite efforts of the two band members to point out that they were gayer than Elton John, more gender-confused than Bruce Jenner, and every bit as committed to social justice, gay pride, queer visibility, female empowerment, breast cancer awareness, Tibetan independence, the European Union, and Black Lives Matter as anyone else, they were rejected by their fellow SJWs faster than a vampire fleeing the approaching rays of the dawn.

The fallout was swift and absolute, with rapid-fire rejections over the next 48 hours: Touring members of the band abruptly quit; several opening bands withdrew from an upcoming tour; Salty Artist Management announced that it had severed ties with PWR BTTM; the Hopscotch Music Festival dropped the band from its lineup; and the record label Polyvinyl released a statement saying that it would no longer be distributing PWR BTTM's music. Father/Daughter Records, which released the band's debut album, followed suit, and by Tuesday, PWR BTTM's music was no longer available on iTunes or Apple Music. Polyvinyl confirmed that the band's distributors had requested that its music be removed from streaming services and online retailers.

"There is absolutely no place in the world for hate, violence, abuse, discrimination or predatory behavior of any kind," Polyvinyl said in its statement. "In keeping with this philosophy, we want to let everyone know that we are ceasing to sell and distribute PWR BTTM's music." The company added that it would refund purchases of "Pageant" and make donations to nonprofit organizations that support victims of sexual abuse and LGBTQ-related violence....

The speed and severity of the response may have surprised some—particularly in the absence of an identified accuser or an official complaint—but the queer punk community has learned, over the years, practices of acceptance and support for its most vulnerable and marginalized members, who often don't feel safe reporting an assault or violation to authorities.

—"Last week, PWR BTTM was the Next Big Thing in punk. Now the band is in ruins, and fans are reeling",
Washington Post, 16 May 2017

The rapid decline and fall of PWR BTTM should suffice to demonstrate the utter mercilessness of the social justice warriors when it comes to those who violate the Narrative in even the smallest of ways. Contrary to the average person's understanding, the more successful you are, the more vicious they will be when they turn on you. SJWs have neither friends nor allies, and they do not hesitate to turn on each other in a heartbeat.

Chapter 5

The SJW Convergence Sequence

In *SJWs Always Lie*, I described the conventional SJW attack sequence. It is an eight-step routine that can be easily observed in most public SJW attacks on individuals. This attack sequence is based upon the foundation of a narrative defined by the SJW and is intended to validate that narrative while publicly demonstrating the SJW's power over his target. The sequence is the practical implementation of Rule 12 of Saul Alinsky's *Rules for Radicals*.

RULE 12: Pick the target, freeze it, personalize it, and polarize it. Cut off the support network and isolate the target from sympathy. Go after people and not institutions; people hurt faster than institutions. (This is cruel, but very effective. Direct, personalized criticism and ridicule works.)

The eight stages of the SJW attack sequence are as follows:

1. Locate or Create a Violation of the Narrative.

2. Point and Shriek.

3. Isolate and Swarm.

4. Reject and Transform.

5. Press for Surrender.

6. Appeal to Amenable Authority.

7. Show Trial.

8. Victory Parade.

In like manner, the convergence of institutions tends to follow a recognizable pattern that operates in much the same way as the SJW attack sequence, but on a larger scale. This pattern can be usefully described as the SJW convergence sequence. We can see how it has played out for the last sixty years in fully converged institutions such as academia, the mainstream media, and the publishing industry, we can see how it plays out today in partially converged institutions such as corporate America and the various Christian churches, and we can see how rapidly the cancer can metastasize in institutions that are just being infiltrated today, such as the game industry and the open source software community.

Regardless of the nature of the institution, the same general pattern of behavior is reliably followed to such an extent that it is relatively easy to identify how badly an institution is converged, and its resultant ability or inability to perform its primary purpose, on the basis of what stage in the convergence sequence has been reached by the SJWs converging it.

For example, when I read the bizarre story of the sudden decline of a once-popular church near my childhood home in Minnesota being reduced to 800 people meeting in a hotel, I knew without even needing to ask anyone what had happened. The church, a Lutheran church called North Heights that my parents had attended in the 1990s, had been infiltrated by SJWs, converged, lost its ability to perform its primary function as a Christian church, and found itself on the brink of failure. What was astonishing to me was just how fast what looked like a rock-solid community institution had gone downhill and collapsed.

Founded in 1946, the church was a fixture in the northern suburbs of St. Paul, with two locations offering seven worship services to 7,000 parishioners. It was one of Minnesota's first megachurches, which always struck me as a little ironic as the senior pastor since 1961, a quiet, humble Scandinavian man named Morris Vaagenes, could not have been further from the smooth, slick-haired Joel Osteen clones that one tends to picture when one thinks of a megachurch. While I seldom attended it, preferring Greg Boyd's Woodland Hills instead, my mother sang in the Christmas choir there, my aunt and uncle and cousins were members, and if I recall correctly, several of my friends' children attended North Heights Christian Academy, a private K-8 Christian school that was founded by the church. It was a church full of good, decent people, nice Minnesota Lutherans in whom even Garrison Keillor could find no fault, who loved Jesus, loved their fellow man, and liked nothing better than to send their children to Haiti or Trinidad for two weeks in the winter to build homes and churches for the less fortunate. It was a wealthy church, too, located as it was near the lake homes of Shoreview and North Oaks, and the parking lot was always filled with Audis, and BMWs, and Mercedes.

Pastor Vaagenes was a genuine man of God, who initially appeared a little weak and bumbling in person, but grew in stature in the pulpit, preaching straight from the Bible with a powerful evangelical fervor that belied his traditional white robes and otherwise unprepossessing demeanor. However, he retired in 1999, and as is so often the case when a strong leader retires, was succeeded by men who were considerably less capable of assuming the burden of leadership. In 2007, a woman by the name of Mindy Bak joined what had become a bloated 88-person staff, and with the help of other SJWs who had also infiltrated the church, managed to get herself appointed interim senior pastor in 2014 through a series of highly political machinations circumventing the traditionalists on the church's Board of Elders. This was rather a remarkable accomplishment, considering that a considerable percentage of the church members were relatively traditional Christians who held to the conventional Biblical teachings on the proper roles of men and women in church ministry.

It was arguably even more remarkable that within just 18 months, attendance had fallen nearly 80 percent, over half the staff was laid off, both total and per-capita giving drastically declined, and the original location was shut down, in part due to "a lack of elevator access for the disabled."

What could possibly motivate a pastor, even a female one, to destroy her own church in this manner? According to one former member quoted in the *Star Tribune*, the answer is pretty simple. "She hates men."

And on March 13, 2016, less than two years after she had been appointed interim senior pastor, Mindy Bak presided over the final service at North Heights Lutheran in front of the last 900 members of the congregation. Her work was done, and what for sixty years was a thriving church community had been destroyed.

> *A long-running schism proves fatal to North Heights Lutheran... Prejudice, sexism and scapegoating all played a role in the church's downfall, Bak said. Members of the breakaway group didn't want a female leader, Bak said, particularly one that didn't shy away from issues that predecessors had refused to address. They didn't want to hear about the prejudices of North Heights or the truth about its finances, she said. Nor did they want to embrace her message that to love Christ you must love even those people who are challenging to love. A sign in the church hall read, in part, "Throughout our history, many grew to be the followers of Jesus we were called to be. But our willingness to love one another, in spite of division, never came. For decades upon decades, selfishness and pride have brought us to this place of self-destruction. We are a cautionary tale of a dying church."*

> ——"Deep divide dooms onetime megachurch North
> Heights Lutheran", *Star Tribune*, 13 March 2016

The convergence, decline, and fall of North Heights Lutheran is indeed a cautionary tale. But it is vital to remember that the SJW convergence of North Heights did not begin with the ascendance of Mindy Bak to the interim senior pastorship. Nor did it begin when she began working at the church in 2007; the fact that she was hired as a pastor indicates that the convergence actually began in the late 1990s, when the church failed to successfully vet its new employees, pastors, and elders. By the time the convergence is visible to the average member of the institution, it is usually too late to salvage the institution in the absence of a strong leader who understands what is at stake, does not fear conflict, and is willing to stand up to the vicious slander and underhanded tactics that will be unleashed against him.

The Organizational Convergence Sequence

Stage One: Infiltration

The infiltration stage usually begins when an institution is at its peak. While it is not unheard of for SJWs to attempt to infiltrate up-and-coming institutions, particularly those in glamorous or trendy industries, the usual pattern is for the SJW to seek out healthy, successful organizations into which they can safely burrow. This is necessary because SJWs are very seldom capable of pretending to be productive employees for very long, particularly in any area of responsibility where the metrics are objective and their inability to perform quickly becomes apparent to their managers and coworkers. This lack of competence is why SJWs are vehemently opposed to meritocracy, as well as to any system of management or governance that is based on merit or even relies upon objective measures for promotion or compensation. Any job that mostly involves make-work and has no bearing on the day-to-day functioning of the organization is one that will draw SJWs like flies to roadkill, particularly if it is a job that focuses primarily upon some element of social justice such as inclusivity, outreach, or community.

SJWs are particularly drawn to HR in the corporate world and community management in the open source world because these organizational roles tend to combine the two things that SJWs seek most: power over others and an absence of personal responsibility. They can also be found in volunteer roles; SJWs tend to have a lot of time on their hands, and volunteering for the jobs that no one else wants to do is one of their favorite ways to make themselves appear indispensable to those who are in charge of the organization. Of course, SJWs are not the only helpful individuals whose assistance can prove undesirable; one churchgoer told me an amusing story of a woman who had been assisting with the Sunday School at his church for some time, who volunteered to take on the responsibility of decorating the church for the holidays when no one else stepped forward. After she unveiled her enthusiastic plans, it took some degree of tact to explain to her that Harry Potter and wizards were not an appropriate theme for a Christian holiday. But if you want to identify the initial SJW in an organization, look for a longtime volunteer, usually female, who is quiet, selfless, well-regarded by everyone, and heavily relied upon by the leadership.

Don't expect SJW infiltrators to be blue-haired, frothing-mad genderqueer activists with thick-framed eyeglasses. And don't expect them to unleash the usual monologues on equality, inclusivity, and the inchoate evil of straight white men on unsuspecting strangers either. SJW infiltrators instinctively understand the need to keep their views to themselves. The initial infiltrator is almost invariably going to be the exception, the woman who is just like one of the guys, the black man who doesn't have a racial chip on his shoulder, or the gay guy who prefers beer and football to methamphetamine-fueled all-night raves. He, or in most cases, she, is going to present as a generally normal individual, who just happens to be a little more quietly liberal than the organizational norm.

Sometimes the infiltration is incidental. SJWs need jobs just like anyone else, after all, and they are more than willing to exploit the well-known tendency of the average white employer to want to score affirmative action points or pick up a get-out-of-sexism-free card by hiring a woman, particularly for a job in a heavily male occupation. This inexplicable temptation to knowingly hire less-qualified candidates the employer knows will probably not fit in well with the existing employees is a form of what I think of as Republican Candidate Syndrome. The connection may not seem immediately apparent, but bear with me because it actually makes sense.

Now, have you ever noticed that in recent U.S. presidential election cycles, in the early stages of the campaign for the Republican nomination, a woefully unqualified and unlikely candidate whom no one has ever heard of not only announces that he is running for president as a Republican but also does inexplicably well in the early caucuses and primaries? In 2015, it was Ben Carson, a neurosurgeon. Four years before, it was Herman Cain, a former CEO and Federal Reserve banker. Before that, the token black candidate was Alan Keyes, an ambassador to the United Nations, who ran for the Republican nomination in 1992, 1996, 2000, and 2008. Now, my family was heavily involved in Republican politics when I was a teenager, and I cannot tell you how many times I heard Republicans declare how much they would absolutely love to vote for a well-spoken black man like Carson, or Cain, or Keyes, for President. Some Republicans, like former Reagan speechwriter Peggy Noonan, got so carried away by Republican Candidate Syndrome that they voted for Barack Obama despite him being a Democrat.

Of course, these Republicans are motivated by nothing more than the desire to signal their virtue and obtain a get-out-of-racism-free card. After all, how can you accuse someone of being racist when he voted for a black man for President? And, of course, the entire exercise turns out to be pure political theater, as futile as the Congressional debt ceiling and as predictable as kabuki. In fact, it is so predictable that you can expect to reliably win money on the prediction sites by betting that the token black Republican candidate will overperform in the early straw polls, then unexpectedly underperform once the primaries start in earnest.

This same desire to virtue-signal, to morally parade one's social self-righteousness, is also observable in corporate America. The desire to vote for a totally unqualified candidate simply because he is black is no different than the desire to hire a programmer for being a woman or any other minority simply due to his minority status. It is an expression of personal magnanimity, of a generousness of spirit that sets one apart from all the other straight white men who would be so shortsighted as to simply vote, or hire, on the basis of perceived merit and ability.

While there are a whole host of intellectual justifications that have been invented over the years to justify the various forms of affirmative action—indeed, there are entire fields of study now devoted to manufacturing new justifications for the preferential treatment of minorities and searching for evidence to continue appealing to the old reasons—they are not relevant to our purpose of understanding the infiltration stage. What does matter is to understand that this desire to virtue-signal exists in many people, and more importantly, to understand that the minorities it benefits not only know that it exists but are fully aware that it is in their interest to appeal to it.

Stage Two: Reinforcement

I got a strange message on Twitter. Someone at GitHub wanted to talk to me. I thought I knew what it was about: a year before, I had been talking to a diversity consultant (who was contracting there at the time) about working with GitHub on diversity and inclusivity and exploring their interest in adopting the Contributor

Covenant across all of their open source projects. But that's not what they wanted this time. They wanted to offer me a job. They had just created a team called Community & Safety, charged with making GitHub more safe for marginalized people and creating features for project owners to better manage their communities.

At first I had my doubts. I was well aware of GitHub's very problematic past, from its promotion of meritocracy in place of a management system to the horrible treatment and abuse of its female employees and other people from diverse backgrounds. I myself had experienced harassment on GitHub. As an example, a couple of years ago someone created a dozen repositories with racist names and added me to the repos, so my GitHub profile had racial slurs on it until their support team got around to shutting them down a few days after I reported the incident. I didn't get the sense that the company really cared about harassment.

My contact at GitHub insisted that the company was transforming itself. She pointed to a Business Insider article that described the culture changes that they were going through, and touted the hiring of Nicole Sanchez to an executive position leading a new Social Impact team. I was encouraged to talk to some other prominent activists that had recently been hired. Slowly, I opened my mind to the possibility. Given my work in trying to make open source more inclusive and welcoming, what could give me more influence in creating better communities than working at the very center of the open source universe?

With these thoughts in mind, I agreed to interview with the team. The code challenge was comparable to other places where I'd interviewed, as was the pairing exercise. I was impressed by the social justice tone of some of the questions that I was asked in the non-technical interviews, and by the fact that the majority of people that

I met with were women. A week later, I had a very generous offer
in hand, which I happily accepted. My team was 5 women and one
man: two of us trans, three women of color.

—"Antisocial Coding: My Year At GitHub",
Coraline Ada Ehmke

As was described in *SJWs Always Lie*, SJWs naturally gravitate to Human Resources for two reasons. First, because it is a job that allows the employee to completely avoid any objective performance standards. How does one measure the performance of an HR employee, or even an HR unit, in objective terms? Any meaningful measure, such as the quality of people interviewed and hired, is intrinsically subjective; this is why most managers can permit themselves to simultaneously believe that their employees are both superior to the industry standard and content to be compensated at industry-standard rates. Avoiding objective performance metrics is always a priority for the SJW because he knows it is much more difficult to spin a narrative that places the responsibility elsewhere when he has specific production targets for which he personally is responsible. The second reason is that Human Resources tends to provide the SJW with maximum influence over the corporation with minimum effort. If you're wondering if there are any SJWs in your company, the first place to check is always HR.

Once securely in place in HR, the SJWs first priority is to hire more SJWs in HR, first in order to provide protective cover to the original SJW, and second to help establish a unit narrative that can begin influencing the corporation as a whole. Once an HR unit is converged, it will begin to regularly transmit propaganda about itself and its activities to the company at large, especially to the executives. There will be a series of programs, initiatives, mandates, and informative broadcasts about new laws and regulations, most of which are of only potential significance to anyone in the company. The more an HR unit communicates to the entire company via email or internal communication system, the more converged you can be certain that it is. These corporate communications usually start in a harmless enough manner, cheerfully letting everyone know that it is Sheryl's birthday today, or the seventh anniversary of Hank joining the corporate family, so if you see them, be sure to wish them a wonderful day!

But before long, they are informing everyone that it is Frida Kahlo's birthday, and if you want to learn more about this great Mexican painter, be sure to sign up for the trip to the local museum next month in time to take advantage of our corporate discount! And gradually, the tone darkens, the exclamation points disappear, and in the place of birthdays and company picnics, dire, Orwellian warnings are issued about behaviors deemed inappropriate, and the outings are transformed into mandatory workshops and seminars. And all the while, they are busily interfering with the attempts of managers to hire productive employees by establishing new corporate policies about job requirements that permit them to weed out anyone who lacks the desired Gender Studies degree or activist profile no matter what the nature of the nominal job is supposed to be.

Over time, the SJWs in HR will transform the corporate culture and make it into the thought police state that is more to their liking, but the cultural transformation always begins in HR. If you are a corporate executive and your company has an HR department, I can guarantee that it is already at least partially converged.

Stage Three: Seize the High Ground

The Twitter Trust and Safety Council provides input on our safety products, policies, and programs. Twitter works with safety advocates, academics, and researchers; grassroots advocacy organizations that rely on Twitter to build movements; and community groups working to prevent abuse.

In corporations and organizations, the high ground is defined as those groups capable of influencing decisions related to hiring, firing, discipline, and compensation. It takes a long time and an amount of proven competence to reach the executive levels, so this is not an option for most SJWs, who can seldom remain in any position requiring objectively measured performance for long. In addition to HR, SJWs have begun to gravitate towards corporate compliance-related jobs, particularly recent inventions like GitHub's Social Impact team. Measuring social impact is the SJW's dream job because it combines not having to do anything substantive with the chance to criticize others, and on top of it all, doing so professionally in the interest of social justice. As you can probably imagine, this is akin to putting the fox in charge of the henhouse and asking it to tell the farmer how many chickens the henhouse needs. No matter what the corporation does, the answer of the Social Impact group will always be the same: it is not enough! There must always be more diversity, more inclusivity, more equality, regardless of any negative potential effects on the company.

Which, of course, are only the figments of the imagination of racist, bigoted, sexist, and outdated white male executives since the SJW can certainly cite no shortage of references and studies to prove that diversity always makes a company stronger, inclusivity always makes a company more productive, and more equality always makes a company more profitable, for reasons that are utterly incomprehensible even when they are coherent.

Groups like the Trust & Safety Council at Twitter and programs such as Google's Diversity Core and Intel's Global Diversity and Inclusion are designed to disrupt the status quo and cement SJW control of the corporation. As the example of James Damore shows, any skepticism about the value of these diversity programs, let alone opposition to them, is crimethink that merits immediate disemployment and public denunciations.

Stage Four: Push for Inclusivity

Every day, we're inundated with more information than we can consciously process. Research shows that simply raising awareness about unconscious bias can lead to more conscious decision making. We started an internal conversation in 2013 about unconscious bias and we continue to invest in unbiasing trainings. Over 74% of Googlers have participated in these workshops, and all new Googlers and managers are trained in it.

—Google Diversity: Inclusion

If you think about the growth of Women's Studies, Black Studies, and other forms of special studies that are now offered as majors at most American universities, you should be able to recognize the sort of make-work job that SJWs always attempt to create for themselves in lieu of doing anything productive or quantifiable. Despite the fact that they provide no functional basis for employment at all, the number of women's and gender studies degrees has grown by more than 300 percent since 1990, and there are now 2,000 such degrees, which is 2,000 more than there were in the first 334 years of higher education in America. And just as the SJW professor who is incapable of teaching math, physics, or even English can preside over a room full of women talking about their feelings or blacks talking about racist white oppression, a woman who cannot write code, provide technical support, or provide basic IT services is perfectly capable of traveling to technology conferences and pontificating about the dire need for more women in Science, Technology, Engineering and Math on behalf of her converged, virtue-signaling employer.

Or leading workshops to train people in unbiasing.

Stage Five: Target the Dissidents

Finally in January I got the chance to work on the one feature that I wanted GitHub to have most of all: a tool to make adding a code of conduct to a project easy. After an initial proof of concept, I worked closely with the team's UX person to create a very streamlined experience. We had been tracking code of conduct adoptions since the summer of 2016, and seeing growth at a rate of 500 projects per month. I was eager to see this rate increase with the addition of the new tool. The code of conduct adoption feature was launched in May 2017, and was widely praised.

—"Antisocial Coding: My Year At GitHub",
Coraline Ada Ehmke

The two primary weapons utilized by corporate SJWs to marginalize opponents of convergence are the now-ubiquitous Code of Conduct and the Community Committee. While codes of conduct sound sensible enough in theory, in practice they are very vaguely worded documents that serve much the same purpose for the Community Committees responsible for enforcing them that petty traffic laws do for the police. Namely, they permit the Community Committee, which may be named the Steering Committee or even the Code of Conduct Committee, to charge anyone who is insufficiently enthusiastic about the organization's new social justice priorities with Code of Conduct violations. Since both looking at another individual and not looking at another individual can be deemed violations of the vast majority of these codes of conduct, you can probably see how they can be weaponized in order to freeze, isolate, and eliminate opponents.

In practice, codes of conduct are also used to smoke out and identify opposition to the SJWs, as the initial skeptics who are the most able to understand the danger posed by a proposed code of conduct will usually tend to serve as the nexus of the resistance against it.

Stage Six: Expel the Infidels

The Node.js community has again turned against itself, this time over a failed vote to oust a controversial member of the project's technical steering committee (TSC) over alleged code-of-conduct violations.... Vagg, who declined to be interviewed, offended members of the Node community through various online posts. A member of the TSC attempted to move the allegations out of public view, but they're presently available through the Internet Archive. Essentially, among other things, Vagg argued there are downsides to codes of conduct, which seek to shut down harassment and super-sketchy behavior within technical conferences and projects.

—"Node.js forks again—this time it's a war of words over
anti-sex-pest codes of conduct", *The Register*,
24 August 2017

While the nebulous code of conduct rules sometimes prove too nebulous to actual make any charges stick well enough to justify expulsion, the very Kafkaesque nature of the process is usually sufficient to demoralize the dissidents and push them into quitting. After all, how does one defend oneself against a code of conduct violation which is comprised of arguing that there are downsides to the code of conduct? Notice that the controversial member is not charged with either harassment or super-sketchy behavior at conferences, but merely with arguing against something that theoretically seeks to shut down such behaviors.

Of course, quitting is always a mistake, however one tries to justify it to oneself. Quitting is the very outcome for which the SJWs are hoping because it saves them the trouble of trying to concoct a plausible case for disemployment where none exists. As I advise in *SJWs Always Lie*, don't go easily, and take as many of them with you as you can while making the rubble bounce on the way out. Remember, SJWs are cowards, and they have little stamina for extended periods of open conflict. They try to wear their opponents down through insinuation and social pressure, killing them with the death of a thousand cuts rather than via a fair trial followed by an execution.

Stage Seven: Milk the Cow

Until July at the earliest, the foundation behind the GNOME desktop environment will be freezing all expenditure deemed not essential to its running will be frozen, as the foundation has run out of cash reserves. "The issue has been caused by a number of factors," wrote GNOME Foundation board member, Ekaterina Gerasimova in a post to the foundation's mailing list. "These include increased administrative overheads in the last few years due to the increased turnover which has been caused by to the Outreach Program for Women."

—"GNOME bled dry by outreach programs",
ZDNet, 14 April 2014

The basic problem with SJW convergence should be relatively obvious. How does an organization survive when it has successfully expelled the larger part of its most productive employees and replaced the company's business priorities with expensive, unprofitable social justice objectives? The answer is very simple: it doesn't.

SJWs have no idea how to make money beyond convincing people to give it to them. While they are very good at that, as the growth of foundations, professional charities, and government income distribution shows, theirs is a fundamentally parasitical and distribution-focused perspective. And like other economic systems that focus on distribution rather than production, the more influential it becomes, the more certainly it is doomed to failure.

Take YouTube, which is the most SJW-converged Google-owned corporation. They will demonetize literally any video at the drop of a hat, in part because that means YouTube gets to keep all the money it produces from advertisers, but also because their SJWs are so sensitive that they can detect one part of Narrative-questioning in a million. YouTube demonetizes about one percent of their videos on an ongoing basis, Contrast this with Blogger, which is also Google-owned, but is so chill about content that it has suspended precisely two of my 20,136 blog posts in 14 years, both times for DMCA-related claims, one of which was false, which amounts to a percentage that is so low that I can't even read the number on my calculator, but is a lot less than one percent.

And, as I mentioned previously, YouTube did not hesitate to crack down on their most-popular YouTuber, PewDiePie. Why would they behave in such an obviously counterproductive manner? Because they don't have to make money; YouTube loses $2 billion per year.

The fact that most open source contributors are unpaid and the projects don't need to make any money in order to accomplish their objectives is the primary reason that open source has been so rapidly converged in comparison with for-profit corporations. It is also why the absolute breeding ground for SJWs is in the not-for-profit organizations.

Social justice is not profitable, but advocating for social justice most certainly can be. And for the individual of limited talents beyond a capacity for expressing outrage, it is arguably the most profitable profession there is.

Stage Eight: Evade the Blame

I think back on the lack of options I was given in response to my mental health situation and I see a complete lack of empathy. I reflect on the weekly one-on-ones that I had with my manager prior to my review and the positive feedback I was getting, in contrast to the surprise annual review. I consider the journal entries that I made and all the effort I put in on following the PIP and demonstrating my commitment to improving, only to be judged negatively for the most

petty reasons. I think about how I opened up to my manager about
my trauma and was accused of trying to manipulate her feelings....
I see that there was, in fact, a real problem with empathy. But that
problem wasn't mine.

—"Antisocial Coding: My Year At GitHub",
Coraline Ada Ehmke

Given what the reader now knows about social justice warriors, I
doubt it will come as any great surprise to discover that the employment of Coraline Ada Ehmke, the individual perhaps most responsible for the convergence of the open source community due to xis
automating the addition of what should have rightly been known as
the Convergence Covenant to open source projects, did not end well.

You really have to read xis account of xis exit from GitHub, because it is quite possibly the funniest thing an SJW has ever written,
and it is certainly funnier than any SJW comedian today. After an
unexpectedly negative performance review was met with a downward
spiral into an episode of bipolar depression, followed by what appears
to have been a fake attempted suicide attempt, a trip to the emer-
gency room, and an eight-day involuntary commitment to a mental
health institution, Mx. Ehmke returned to xis job and was genuinely
shocked to discover that despite keeping thorough notes, following all
xis checklists, reading and re-reading every written communication to
make sure xis words and tone were above criticism, xe was let go.

The most amusing aspect of Ehmke's firing is the way in which
GitHub apparently did everything short of muzzling Coraline and
strapping xim into the redundant restraints to which serial killer
Garland Green was subjected in *Con Air*, just to get Ehmke safely
out the door without destroying their entire code base or triggering
the core reactor into a meltdown. It's hard to feel much sympathy for
them though. This sort of result was all but inevitable from the time
they established their Social Impact team.

Many corporations, churches, charities, institutions, open source projects, and other organizations now find themselves caught up in the organizational convergence sequence, and in many cases, much further along than the sane members of their organization would like. The good news is that just as GitHub was able to at least partially extricate itself from its great experiment with enforcing social justice on the programmers of the world, SJW convergence is curable, even when it looks as if the organizational cancer is terminal.

No story is ever truly over, but those who find themselves caught in the throes of despair may find encouragement to know how the next chapter in the story of the fatally converged Lutheran church has begun.

About a year after North Heights Lutheran Church briefly closed its doors due to financial issues and disagreements, the church has completely paid off its mortgage and hired a new senior pastor it believes will bring continuing unity. "One of the things that we feel is that the future will be greater than the past," said Rev. Morris Vaagenes of Shoreview, who was the senior pastor of the church from 1961 to 1999. Vaagenes described what the church went through in recent years in Biblical terms. "We had to go through a crucifixion— the death of the old—in order to receive the new," he said. "There can be no resurrection without crucifixion."

—"One year later, buried church rises from tomb of
debt", *Shoreview Press*, 13 June 2017

THE CUSTOM DICTIONARY

CRYING WOLF

THE BAIT AND BAN

NAZI

THE WORST PERSON IN THE WORLD

THE FALSE ALLY

Chapter 6

Standard SJW Tactics

"Take all statements by an SJW about himself as diametrically opposite the truth, and all accusations flung at others to be tacit confessions about himself, their odd and neurotic speech patterns, hypocrisies, and insolent self-contradictions fit into a clear pattern, and can be understood."

—John C. Wright

In July 2017, I was sentenced to Twitter jail. For one week.

It was embarrassing, not because I was the least bit concerned about not having access to social media for one week, but because I had fallen victim to a common SJW tactic only two weeks after warning people not to talk to the media. The timing was also unfortunate, since I had just launched the Daily Meme Wars mailing list with 500 subscribers only a week before. Now, I was perfectly aware that SJWs on Twitter were baiting people into responses that would result in suspensions and bans from Twitter's Trust & Safety Council, and I had been very disciplined about not responding to obvious provocations. But I made the mistake of answering an "innocent" question from a curious individual, which led to a series of increasingly prosecutorial questions that alerted me to the fact that this seemingly innocent party was actually an SJW on the prowl. So, knowing what he was after, I tweeted a wordless response, blocked him, and thought no more of it.

No more until Twitter informed me two days later that my account was partially suspended for a week.

Live and learn. It turns out that even an image of a fish in an oven crosses one of Twitter's arbitrarily drawn lines. This may explain why we don't very often see Nathan Outlaw or Éric Ripert on Twitter.

Twitter jail is a rather fascinating experience due to its psychological sadism. Unlike a proper suspension that completely blocks the user's access to the site, in Twitter jail, the user is granted full access to his account. He can read tweets and navigate Twitter in the normal fashion, but he is not permitted to tweet, retweet, or like the tweets of others. The brilliance of the design (and I like to think it is intentional on the designer's part rather than, as I suspect, simple laziness on the part of the programmers) is that the user is given no visual cues whatsoever that his access has been limited in any way. The icons are all present, they are not grayed-out or otherwise altered in appearance, and best of all, they remain fully functional. However, should the user foolishly conclude that perhaps the announced sentence was a mistake, or that techno-clemency was granted him, and actually click on a working icon to utilize one of the forbidden functions, a window pops up informing him that such an action is in violation of the terms of his suspension and another hour has been added to it.

This adds a lovely, sadistic little twist to the Twitter jail experience, because of course the user does not know precisely when his suspension began. A man may know the season and the day, but only Twitter knows the hour. So, in order to avoid accidentally prolonging his suspension, the average Twitter-convict will voluntarily add a day to his own suspension. Brilliant!

This, of course, is an illustration of the SJW tactic known as bait-and-report, which is frequently encountered on social media sites such as Twitter and Facebook, as well as in the comment sections of blogs and mainstream media sites. It is one of more than a dozen such tactics that I have observed SJWs utilizing over the past few years, and what is fascinating is how many of these tactics were first observed more than 2,400 years ago by one of Man's greatest thinkers, Aristotle.

On SJW Refutations

A lot of SJWs wildly overrate their ability to argue. I like to think that I may have helped a few of them better understand the effective limits of their ability. But at the end of the day, it doesn't really matter what one thinks of one's own ability to argue; what matters is what those who have actually observed one's arguments think of them. In any event, what I find more interesting than a perfectly normal inability to correctly self-assess is how most people are completely unable to expose false arguments despite the fact that the tools for doing so have been readily available for literally thousands of years.

But then, Aristotle understood that for some people, the perception is much more important than the observable reality.

> *"Now for some people it is better worthwhile to seem to be wise, than to be wise without seeming to be (for the art of the sophist is the semblance of wisdom without the reality, and the sophist is one who makes money from an apparent but unreal wisdom); for them, then, it is clearly essential also to seem to accomplish the task of a wise man rather than to accomplish it without seeming to do so."*

Those who have read *SJWs Always Lie* will recall how, in his *Rhetoric*, Aristotle provided us with a guide to the two languages of persuasion, dialectic and rhetoric, and warned us that some individuals are limited to the latter. However, it is another, even more famous work of his that is of interest to us here, as the sixth work of his Organon, as the standard collection of his works on logic are known, provides us with a guide to the understanding the flawed and dishonest foundations of many arguments presented in support of social justice. *De Sophisticis Elenchis*, or *On Sophistical Refutations* as it is more commonly known, details thirteen specific logical fallacies, several of which are habitually committed by SJWs. While more than a few readers have found Aristotle's *Rhetoric* to be a little on the convoluted side, *On Sophistical*

Refutations is relatively straightforward, it's very short, and it is well worth reading as it specifically identifies a number of basic tactics that are repeatedly utilized by those who are presenting invalid arguments, or as is more often the case, presenting a false refutation of another's argument. And Aristotle makes the connection between social justice warriors and sophistry by noting, in *Rhetoric*, that "a man is a sophist because he has a certain kind of moral purpose."

The SJW naturally gravitates towards sophistry because his twisted morality does not recognize association with the truth to be moral, but rather, association with the social justice Narrative.

Aristotle divides the thirteen fallacies he identifies into two sections: those that primarily concern playing word games, and those that do not.

Those ways of producing the false appearance of an argument which depend on language are six in number: they are ambiguity, amphiboly, combination, division of words, accent, form of expression. Of this we may assure ourselves both by induction, and by syllogistic proof based on this-and it may be on other assumptions as well-that this is the number of ways in which we might fail to mean the same thing by the same names or expressions... Refutations, then, that depend upon language are drawn from these common-place rules. Of fallacies, on the other hand, that are independent of language there are seven kinds.

Fallacies in the language

- *Ambiguity*
- *Amphibology*
- *Combination*
- *Division*
- *Accent*
- *Form of expression*

Fallacies not in the language

- *Accident*
- *Secundum quid*
- *Irrelevant conclusion*
- *Begging the question*
- *False cause*
- *Affirming the consequent*
- *Complex question*

Don't be alarmed by the unfamiliar terms. As it happens, if you have ever encountered an SJW, then you are already familiar with many, if not most, of these fallacious argument styles. To begin with one very detailed example, what Aristotle calls ambiguity is simply substituting one definition for another, thereby allowing the SJW to magically transform X into Not-X in order to refute his opponent's argument. Aristotle helpfully provides several examples of this:

Arguments such as the following depend upon ambiguity. 'Those learn who know: for it is those who know their letters who learn the letters dictated to them'. For to 'learn' is ambiguous; it signifies both 'to understand' by the use of knowledge, and also 'to acquire knowledge'. Again, 'Evils are good: for what needs to be is good, and evils must needs be'. For 'what needs to be' has a double meaning: it means what is inevitable, as often is the case with evils, too (for evil of some kind is inevitable), while on the other hand we say of good things as well that they 'need to be'. Moreover, 'The same man is both seated and standing and he is both sick and in health: for it is he who stood up who is standing, and he who is recovering who is in health: but it is the seated man who stood up, and the sick man who was recovering'. For 'The sick man does so and so', or 'has so and so done to him' is not single in meaning: sometimes it means 'the man who is sick or is seated now', sometimes 'the man who was sick formerly'. Of course, the man who was recovering was the sick

*man, who really was sick at the time: but the man who is in health
is not sick at the same time: he is 'the sick man' in the sense not that
he is sick now, but that he was sick formerly.*

To provide a more recent example of an SJW utilizing both ambiguity and amphiboly, in 2015, the SFWA's then-Vice-President,
Mary Robinette Kowal, attempted to refute someone's claim that I
seldom attacked anyone who had not attacked me first. She asserted
the following.

*HA! His first mention of me is mid-2013. He has threatened to post
where I live. And yes, he could, because he has the SFWA directory.
This idea that you can ignore him and he'll go away is demonstrably
not how it works. Speaking as someone who has been the repeated
target of Vox Day, this strategy does not work. Until April 11, 2015,
I have NEVER mentioned him on my blog. EVER. I have him
blocked on all social media.*

Sounds superficially convincing, doesn't it? And yet, this refutation
is sophistical, ambiguous, deceptive, and full of lies.

First, this was my first, and only, mention of her in 2013. I was
using the cover of her recently released novel as an example of the
way in which the science fiction publishers were engaging in their
own deceptive and ambiguous practice of selling romance under the
guise of science fiction and fantasy.

Consider the cover of Mary Robinette Kowal's new novel, Without
A Summer. *Kowal is the current VP of SFWA. She's nice, she's
talented, and she's an award-winning writer. She was even nominated for the Best Novel Nebula in 2010. What she isn't is an
SF/F writer. She's a romance writer. The marketing department
at Tor Books clearly knows that. Both the Handsome Prince and
the Pretty Princess with her bluebirds on the cover are straight out
of Disney. Giving a Nebula award to a book like this would be*

akin to giving Joe Abercrombie the Golden Tea Cosy or whatever
award it is the RWA gives out because one of his mentally unstable
killers happens to tenderly rape a female captive during a momentary
interlude between bloody battles.

That is not exactly the threatening personal attack implied, is it? Second, while it was true that she had never mentioned me on her blog, she had publicly called me out on Twitter, in a flawless example of the amphiboly that Aristotle describes. I prefer to think of it as the SJW's Custom Dictionary. "How can you claim I attacked you when I didn't even punch you? Sure, I kicked you, stabbed you, and elbowed you in the head, but I didn't actually *punch* you." It's an effective way to hide the lie under a veil of partial truth, at least from those who aren't paying sufficiently close attention.

But what about my threat to post where she lives? That's pretty outrageous, is it not? Well, as is usually the case with SJW claims, significant details have been omitted in order to imply the precise opposite of the truth.

You see, the science fiction and fantasy community suffers from a pedophilia problem. It has for decades, ranging from fans and Science Fiction and Fantasy Writers Association members to recognized grandmasters and lifetime achievement award winners. On June 24, 2014, nearly one year after I was supposedly expelled from SFWA for unspecified thought crimes, I noted the fact that 18 years after Ed Kramer's first arrest for aggravated child molestation, 14 years after his arrest on three counts of child molestation, three years after arrest in Connecticut for "risk of injury to a minor," 18 months after being arrested again in Connecticut for violating his bond, and six months after his guilty plea on three counts of child molestation, he was still an active member of SFWA. And to prove this, I cited both the 2010 SFWA directory as well as a screen capture from the SFWA's online member directory taken on June 23, 2014.

And this was the Twitter exchange between Kowal and me.

Mary Robinette Kowal @MaryRobinette
What are these facts you speak of? Such a strange and silly custom

Vox Day @voxday
"Agent Code: (MAA Jackson)". Now, would you like me to put up the entire page 26 scan as evidence, Mary?

Mary Robinette Kowal @MaryRobinette
Scan of what, as evidence of what?

Vox Day @voxday
The facts you questioned: Ed Kramer's membership.

Mary Robinette Kowal @MaryRobinette
In 2010. YOU said he is a current member, which is false.

Now, the point that I was making, and that she knew perfectly well that I was making, was that on page 26 of the 2010 SFWA directory, Ed Kramer was listed directly below one Mary Robinette Kowal, and therefore, posting the page as evidence of his membership would also expose her private address to everyone as well as her telephone number and email address. Because I did not wish to do that, I was pointing out that her demand for evidence of Kramer's membership would necessitate posting where she lived. Of course, being an SJW, she immediately attempted to deceptively portray this desire to avoid posting where she lived as a threat to do so. (This is another standard SJW tactic, Assume the Worst Possible Interpretation.) In doing so, Kowal was attempting to create a false narrative about me attacking her as well as setting up a false dichotomy between the evidence for Kramer being an Active Member in 2010 and his being an Inactive Member in 2014. Moreover, her claim that Kramer was not an active member in 2014 was belied by the SFWA's own online membership directory, which listed Kramer as an active member as late as June 2014.

Only hours after I posted the screenshot proving as much, Ed Kramer abruptly disappeared from the SFWA membership directory. The truth is that Ed Kramer remains an inactive current member of SFWA despite his multiple arrests and convictions for molesting children; the only reason he is inactive is that he was unable to pay his annual membership dues from prison. To the best of my knowledge, the SFWA Board has never voted to expel Ed Kramer, it has never issued a public or private statement about him, and the organization has never announced his expulsion. To the contrary, many of SFWA's members, including some of its more famous ones, have publicly defended him, even in SFWA publications. At no time was he, or the late Marion Zimmer Bradley, or the Marion Zimmer Bradley estate which is still listed on the SFWA's Estate Contact Information page, ever subject to any organizational discipline for their documented sexual crimes against children.

Aristotelian ambiguity is a tactic that is often used by SJWs claiming the right to assign to their opponent the only possible meaning of a word that the opponent has used, even when the other meanings of that word are much more readily applicable and the opponent has declared that the assigned meaning was not the meaning utilized. The fact that this requires both mind-reading and the opponent's ignorance of his own word-choice seldom slows the SJW down because SJWs are always intellectually dishonest.

Word Games

Given the size of this book, it is not practical to go into similar detail with regard to every sophistical refutation and related SJW tactic, but we can at least list them along with an explanation and a brief example of each. Fallacies in the language is simply another way of saying that the SJW is playing word games. Of the six classic examples delineated by Aristotle, five of them are utilized on a regular basis by social justice warriors.

Ambiguity we have already described. It can be created by switching one word for another, by leaving a false impression through implication, or by substituting an irrelevant definition of one word for the relevant one. I tend to think of it as the *Bait-and-Switch*, or *Every Richard Dawkins Argument Ever*. You, however, might find it easier to remember as the *Humpty Dumpty Dictionary*: "When I use a word," Humpty Dumpty said, in rather a scornful tone, "it means just what I choose it to mean—neither more nor less." It is worth noting in this regard that SJWs who favor ambiguity-based refutations are extremely vulnerable to having their own tactics used against them. By intentionally utilizing a word that has multiple definitions, including some that are less than helpful to your case, you can be certain that the SJW will latch onto the definition he perceives to be most damaging to your argument and thereby leap eagerly into the trap. SJWs will reliably do so because their objectives in an argument are usually focused on disqualifying their opponents in the eyes of the crowd rather than in genuinely refuting their arguments. Once the SJW has attacked the wrong definition, it is then a simple matter to turn the table by providing the correct one and discrediting him in the process.

Amphiboly is related to ambiguity. In fact, the word stems from the same Greek root, *ampho*, which means "two sides". However, it involves ambiguity that is created from a sentence can be interpreted in various ways due to grammar, structure, or punctuation. Amphiboly applies when the context that is necessary to understand the statement is removed or left out, such as the fact that while Kowal had NEVER EVER mentioned me *on her blog*, she had addressed me directly on Twitter and mentioned me in the SFWA's private forums. Amphiboly can a difficult word to remember since it tends to leave one with the vague impression that it has something to do with frogs, so I remember it as being the Case of the Missing Context.

Combination is a particular favorite of SJWs in the media. Combination occurs when an SJW claims that because something is true of some part of the whole, it is therefore true of the whole. We see this all the time from SJWs, such as when one Nazi flag at Charlottesville is taken as conclusive evidence that the entire Alt-Right is dedicated to the 25 unalterable points of the German National Socialist Workers' Party's Munich Manifesto, or when a group of white sorority girls singing along to a Kanye West song is cited as proof that all white people are racists who want to re-enslave black Americans. SJWs tend to naturally think in terms of combination, which is why you will almost always search in vain for any mention of a Democratic politician's party membership when he is arrested and accused of a crime, while in the case of a Republican lawmaker, his party membership will usually lead the headline. You can perhaps remember this as *The Specific is the General*. Or, if you are a wargamer of a certain age, as *Pacific General*.

Division is the exact opposite of Combination. This fallacy is much less popular with SJWs than Combination, but it is seen from time to time when they venture forth into the unfamiliar territory of statistical analysis, particularly as it relates to race. For example, any observation that the average IQ of blacks is 85, one standard deviation below that of whites, will inevitably cause the SJW to declare that the observer believes all blacks are stupid, never mind the fact that this observation, combined with a standard bell curve distribution and the global population, means that there are 231.7 million individuals of African descent who are more intelligent than the average white individual. As it is the converse of Combination, you can remember Division as *The General is the Specific*.

Accent is not much used by SJWs or anyone else who speaks English because it is defined as "the ambiguity that emerges when a word can be mistaken for another by changing suprasegmental phonemes, which in Ancient Greek correspond to diacritics." Also known as prosody, it is almost entirely irrelevant today, even in its expanded form that is based on the stress one lays on an individual word. You can safely ignore this one.

Form of expression is also known as the figure-of-speech fallacy. This is not uncommon among SJWs, particularly those who are attempting to play the gotcha game in order to discredit or disqualify someone. However, it is probably better described as a category error, since the Aristotelian example concerns putting words in the wrong categories, such as erroneously putting an adjective, which describes quality, in the verb category, which describes action. Aristotle considered the confusion of categories to be the chief cause of metaphysical mistakes, which tends to suggest that category errors on the part of SJWs may well be unintentional, as they are clearly metaphysically challenged. The phrase often used by scientists, that an idea is "not even wrong," is often applicable here, as category errors tend to render a statement ridiculous and irrelevant as well as incorrect. That being said, some form-of-expression fallacies are clearly intentional. It is almost certainly an intentional category error when objections to mass Islamic immigration into the European Union are described by SJWs as being racist, for the obvious reason that Islam is a religion, not a race or an ethnicity, and even the most maleducated SJW is likely to know that.

Logic Games

In addition to the six classic word games that Aristotle identifies, there are seven fallacies that are based in logic rather than language, all of which are arrows in the SJW arsenal. As Stefan Molyneux, author of the philosophical bestseller *The Art of the Argument*, has said, trying to have a reasonable debate with a Leftist is like trying to nail Jell-O to the wall, so it is useful to know these basic fallacies well enough to be able to identify them when you encounter them, as you inevitably will. And it is a powerful showstopper to correctly call out the specific fallacy being committed, particularly if you follow that up with an interrogation focused on learning whether the SJW is knowingly relying upon it or not. Once the debate turns into a discussion of whether the SJW is being deceitful or is merely ignorant, it's all over but for the SJW running away crying.

Accident is simply ignoring the obvious exception to the rule by attempting to apply a general rule to a situation where it is not relevant. Accident is the favored fallacy of the Black Lives Matter group, which exists mostly on the basis of a textbook example of it.

- Shooting and killing blacks is racist.

- The police shoot and kill blacks.

- Therefore, the police are racist.

You can perhaps remember the accident fallacy more easily if you think of it as the *Valid Exception.*

Secundum quid sounds complicated, but it is actually nothing more than when the SJW refuses to recognize the difference between general rules with exceptions and rules that hold universally true that have no exceptions. Also known more usefully as *Destroying the Rule*, it is the converse of the Valid Exception and involves attempting to claim, on the basis of the exception, that the rule does not exist at all. Example: "Did you see hear that someone painted a swastika on the building? That means that the university administration is run by Nazis!" SJWs often use Destroying the Rule as an attempt to falsely impute hypocrisy or to claim that a failure to meet a moral standard is indicative of the fact that the standard does not exist, and more insidiously, they also create fake hate crimes and commit other hoaxes in order to appeal to it.

Irrelevant conclusion should be self-explanatory, but it is formally defined as an argument that does not address the issue in question, regardless of whether the argument happens to be valid or not. We are informed that it is also known as missing the point, which effectively describes so many SJW arguments as to almost render the description useless. Indeed, it would be surprising if an analysis of the SJW arguments presented on social media did not find that a majority of SJW arguments commit this fallacy. It literally took me less than five seconds to find a fine example of what is formally known as *ignoratio elenchi* on Twitter by going to the President's Twitter account.

> *Donald J. Trump @realDonaldTrump*
> *If NFL fans refuse to go to games until players stop disrespecting our Flag & Country, you will see change take place fast. Fire or suspend!*

> *Ed Krassenstein @EdKrassen 4h4 hours ago*
> *If America unfollows you on Twitter, we wouldn't have to listen to a madman bickering first thing each morning!*

> *Ed Krassenstein @EdKrassen*
> *The First Amendment protects protests, but it doesn't protect blocking people on Twitter. You are a hypocrite #takeaknee*

> *Ed Krassenstein @EdKrassen 4h4 hours ago*
> *The First Amendment also doesn't protect rigging an election!*

This is almost certainly the most common fallacy to which social justice warriors are prone, as the greater part of SJW responses to statements and arguments fall into this category. Even when other common fallacies, such as Ambiguity and the Humpty Dumpty Dictionary, are utilized, they are often used in combination with Missing the Point.

Begging the question is when the SJW has reached a conclusion on the basis of a premise that lacks support. Merriam-Webster claims that *Assume the Conclusion* would be a more accurate translation of *petitio principii* (itself a Medieval Latin translation of the Aristotelian phrase). A common form of Assuming the Conclusion is circular reasoning, which is when the SJW assumes the truth of his argument's conclusion as part of the premises on which he is basing the argument, but the reasoning does not have to be circular in order for the error to qualify as begging the question. Regardless, begging the question does NOT mean to cause the question to be raised, as it is sometimes erroneously used, and as at least one SJW-converged dictionary is attempting to redefine it. It is very, very common for SJWs to Assume the Conclusion, in both circular and non-circular forms, especially when making accusations of racism, sexism, and homophobia, where any denial of the charge is deemed to be evidence of its truth.

False cause is precisely what it sounds like: assigning an incorrect cause to an event that is actually caused by something else. This fallacy is very frequently committed by SJWs when science is under discussion. Indeed, one could quite reasonably argue that the entire discipline of social science exists on the basis of this fallacy. Three oft-heard examples of False Cause are when SJWs attribute crime to poverty or a lack of education, attempt to claim differences in average family income are the source of divergent average group performances on the Scholastic Aptitude Test, and blame global warming on human activity.

Affirming the consequent is a formal fallacy that is considerably less often encountered, although a crude and unsophisticated version of it that I call *That Just Proves* is utilized as a form of rhetoric by some SJWs. Another, more useful description is the confusion of necessity and sufficiency, which occurs when one infers the opposite from the original statement. To put it more simply, if X implies Y, that does not mean that Not-X necessarily is Not-Y. It might be, but it also might not be, so to say that it is would be wrong. Since it's very unlikely that you will encounter this form of argument from an SJW or be able to coherently explain to him what is false about it, let's just move on.

Complex question is a technical term for what in practical terms is usually encountered as the *Loaded Question*. There is more to it than that in formal logic, but the Loaded Question is the form in which it is usually utilized by SJWs. A question is loaded when an SJW asks a question that assumes something that has either not been proven or has not been accepted by the other party. For example, when an SJW demands to know if you are racist or a white supremacist, he is asking a loaded and fallacious question because it artificially restricts the possible responses to being one or the other, when in fact one could be either, both, or neither.

A Catalog of SJW Tactics

In my early encounters with SJWs in the science fiction community, I began to notice a pattern of similar behaviors across a fairly wide range of individuals. As those who have read *SJWs Always Lie* will recall, the SJW with whom I had the most frequent run-ins was John Scalzi, the science fiction writer who is published by Tor Books. In 2013, I happened to witness his encounter with another individual and observed that he hadn't changed what passes for his debating technique since at least 2005.

- Make an obviously questionable assertion.

- When the assertion is questioned, appeal to bachelor's degree in philosophy of language from the University of Chicago.

- When the appeal to the bachelor's degree is questioned, question the questioner's intellect and/or good will.

- Avoid further questions.

- Posture as if one has thoroughly proved one's point.

Not long after this, a reader mentioned that he, too, had noticed the same strange pattern of behavior. He described a long argument he had with Scalzi where the writer had insulted him over and over again, failed to read a single post he wrote, argued against strawmen, and demonstrated what the reader described as a disturbing ignorance of what most people actually believe. And, to put the icing on the cake, Scalzi even threw around the mighty weight of his academic credentials, the aforementioned bachelor's degree, which entirely failed to impress the reader, who happened to possess a master's degree in philosophy himself.

That was when I realized that SJWs tend to utilize the exact same tactics over and over again, and even repeat the very same arguments, no matter with whom they are arguing or what the subject is. They like to pose as if they are intelligent and well-educated, and they often possess academic credentials of one sort or another, but they are observably incompetent as well as dishonest and intentionally deceptive. Most of them exhibit what is described as the Dunning-Kruger effect, which, in accordance with the Third Law of Social Justice, they not infrequently attempt to impute to their opponents.

Dunning and Kruger explained that incompetent people tend to overestimate their own level of skill, fail to recognize genuine skill in others, and fail to recognize the extent of their own inadequacy. This is frequently true of social justice warriors, as they prefer to place their faith in credentials and successful posturing instead of material achievement and successful demonstrations of competence.

Over the years, I have encountered literally hundreds of social justice warriors, great and small, from famous authors and media stars to Internet nobodies, and in that time I have mentally noted a number of the tactics and techniques I have seen them utilize. This is a list of the tactics, both individual and organizational, that they commonly use, which will help you anticipate and prepare for their actions.

THE PROMOTION

THE MOVE ON

THE FIGHT PROMOTION

THE BRAVE SIR ROBIN

Individual Tactics

The Tag Team: If you take down an SJWs argument with dialectic and successfully explain why his position makes absolutely no sense under any circumstances, he'll disappear, but another SJW will promptly show up to attack your position from a different direction.

The Brave Sir Robin: When overmatched, the SJW will run away and declare victory.

The Dog Pile: If triggered by a rhetorical response to his own attack, the SJW will broadcast it as far and wide as he can in order to summon reinforcements. This tactic is also known as the Swarm, and is the desired result of the Point-and-Shriek.

The Bait and Ban: The SJW attempts to draw you into a discussion, often by asking seemingly innocent questions or pretending to be seeking information about something that he's just heard about. His questions will increasingly turn prosecutorial, then devolve into outright attacks. If you respond, he will try to amplify your responses until he has something that he can take to the relevant authorities in order to get you fired or kicked off the social media site.

DARVO: This stands for Deny, Attack, and Reverse Victim and Offender. Often used by sexual offenders who project their own crimes onto their victims, SJWs frequently resort to this tactic when they are playing the victim. When the SFWA Board voted to expel me for using an unofficial Twitter account to link to an attack on another member on my blog, they pretended to be unaware that I had a) been publicly slandered by the "victim" at her Guest of Honor speech at a science fiction convention, and b) that SFWA members had linked to that attack on me, a fellow member, in the SFWA's own forums. One of those members was the President, who was a member of the Board that voted to expel me despite being guilty himself of the "crime" of which I was falsely accused.

Crying Wolf: When an SJW is feeling overmatched, or is responded to rhetorically in kind, he will often make false claims of abuse, harassment, and stalking. This is particularly common if the SJW is female or black.

The Move On: When the SJW helpfully tries to get you to just admit you made a mistake so everyone can move on. This, of course, is similar to the "all we want is an apology" tactic, and any admission of guilt will result in the SJW moving on to the prosecution stage.

The Custom Dictionary: This is the same as Aristotle's Ambiguity, or the Humpty Dumpty Dictionary, in which the SJW selects, or utilizes, whatever definition he finds most useful to his cause at the moment, regardless of what you actually meant.

The Gatling Gun: The SJW spams you with insults until he finds one he believes triggers you or makes you look sufficiently bad to others. This doesn't necessarily mean one that actually serves either purpose, which can be confusing.

The Woodstock 1969: The SJW claims you were at a place, did something, or had a conversation that could have never taken place. The more outlandish the claim, the more effective this tactic is because it tends to confuse the target, and it can be difficult to convincingly disprove a negative, especially when the accusation is coming from a stranger on the Internet. The aim is to discredit and disqualify the target.

The Planted Seed: This is when the SJW intentionally plants a false claim with the aim of getting enough of their allies in the media or high visibility sites to repeat it. The ultimate goal is to get it repeated by a media outlet considered a reliable source by Wikipedia. Once it does, the false claim becomes a part of the official narrative. As a result of my very successful 2015 Rabid Puppies campaign, I have had this tactic used against me, which resulted in Mike VanHelder of *Popular Science* writing "Big winner Vox Day is an outspoken white supremacist", which led to false claims of my being a white supremacist being repeated by Jeet Heer of the *New Republic*, Olivia Nuzzi of *New York Magazine*, and eventually, Wikipedia. As of September 1, 2017, the Wikipedia entry about me includes this Planted Seed:

Writing for Publishers Weekly, *Kimberly Winston described Day as a "fundamentalist Southern Baptist", but other journalists have made more pointed characterizations, such as Mike VanHelder's assertion in* Popular Science *that Day's views are "white supremacist."*

False De-escalation: When the SJW feels that he is losing the rhetorical argument or the sympathy of the onlookers, he may falsely assume a conciliatory position. This is not genuine, and he will return to the attack whenever he feels the situation is more favorable to him.

The Worst Person in the World: This is *MSNBC* anchor Keith Olbermann's shtick, but SJWs seem to feel that it is effective. The SJW claims you are "worse than Hitler" due to your violation of the Narrative, at least until the next worst person in the world comes along.

The False Ally: One SJW pretends to take your side while the other SJW presents the SJW case. The first SJW then pretends to be convinced and demands to know how you could fail to be similarly convinced. He acts betrayed when you fail to go along with his sudden conversion.

Attack the Family: SJWs will always go after your wife and children. Many SJWs are sexual deviants, even more are incapable of maintaining long term relationships, and most are childless, so they have none of the normal restraints that have caused people over the centuries to regard families as being off-limits. The fury of the target's response and the complete lack of sympathy for the SJW from third parties often leaves the SJW reeling in confusion.

The Promotion: SJWs always attempt to elevate a leader of the opposition in order to freeze, isolate, and marginalize him, thereby weakening the opposition. It is almost comical to observe how many times the #1 Amazon bestselling author and former *Breitbart Tech* editor Milo Yiannopoulos has been promoted to the leadership of the Alt-Right by SJWs in the media, despite his sole contribution to the Alt-Right being the co-authorship of one of the first media pieces about it.

The Fight Promoter: There is nothing SJWs like better than "let's you and him fight." SJWs always seek to sow miscommunication and disagreement between their opponents. If Mike Cernovich, Stefan Molyneux, or Paul Joseph Watson say something that can somehow be taken as a disagreement with me, I always hear about it right away from SJWs eager to promote a fight between us.

The Challenging Assertion: This is when the SJW makes a statement of opinion presented as fact, daring you to contradict it and thereby reveal yourself as a Narrative-denier and legitimate target for the SJW. SJWs often like to use this tactic in order to start political arguments at family gatherings. It is particularly effective in social situations where conflict is uncomfortable because, knowing that the SJW is the unreasonable party, the moderates almost invariably side against whoever takes up the gauntlet. It is also used in combination with The Predicted Demise in an attempt to demoralize opponents.

It's Just This One Brick: SJWs always defend the next tactical step towards their long-term objective as being totally unrelated to all their past and future efforts. Apparently, they believe their opponents are too clueless to realize that the wall they are constructing with those bricks is visible to the observer. In fairness, this approach does seem to work very well with moderates, who are always eager to end an impasse by giving the SJWs what they demand.

The False Fallacy: SJWs are limited to the use of rhetoric, but the more intelligent ones recognize the power of dialectic and attempt to use pseudo-dialectic to impress those unable to distinguish between it and the real thing. When confronted, they will often claim the opponent has made a logical fallacy, although when asked which specific fallacy was made, not only are they unable to identify it, they cannot even point out where in the argument it occurs. Another variant of this is the *Ad Humbug*, which is when the SJW confuses a straightforward insult with an actual Ad Hominem argument. Neither "You're stupid" nor "Your argument is wrong and you are stupid" are ad hominem. "Your argument is wrong BECAUSE you're racist" is an example of an actual argumentum ad hominem, which, of course, is a typical SJW argument.

Andrew Flick @AndrewFlick87
So many logical fallacies here.

Supreme Dark Lord @voxday
Name them. Specifically. Is it Ambiguity, Amphiboly, Combination, Division... wait, is it Accent?

Andrew Flick @AndrewFlick87
Btw False equivalence is a logical fallacy in which two opposing arguments appear to be logically equivalent when they are not.

Supreme Dark Lord @voxday
That does not apply here. Where does the equivalence fail? Moreover, you said there were "so many" logical fallacies. How many, eight?

Andrew Flick @AndrewFlick87
Promoting hate speech and promoting upholding of civil rights are

not equivalent. Also, suck a big fat cock and choke on it. Have a nice day

The Straw Man's Advocate: The SJW assumes a position for his opponent, then pontificates on how this assumed position is contrary to something that the opponent has said, creating a hitherto nonexistent dichotomy between the opponent's two positions. Any failure to rectify the real position with the imaginary one is proof that the opponent is wrong and a hypocrite. *Example*: "I am sure you would agree that racism is bad. Can't you see your position is racist?"

The Straw Man's Mask: This is when the SJW incorrectly summarizes the opponent's position in order to better attack it. This tactic is almost invariably presented with weasel words such as "it appears", "it seems", or "apparently". The following is an actual quote from an SJW on Twitter in a discussion about the NFL national anthem protests. *Example:* "It appears you're admitting to being a Nazi based on your reasoning."

The Failed Flounce: When feeling pressed, SJWs frequently declare that they are too busy to continue the discussion or have to leave for one reason or another. More often than not, this does not prevent them from continuing the argument for another hour or two.

The Forgetful Fade: Upon being confronted with an opponent who outmatches them, an SJW will often vanish, only to return again later with precisely the same arguments, facts, and figures that were previously refuted.

Attack the Source: SJWs frequently request a source for even the most obviously true statement in order to attack it rather than argue the point directly or admit they are wrong. This tactic is so frequently utilized by SJWs that I now ignore all requests for sources and automatically delete or block anyone who requests a source more than once.

The Sock Puppet: This is when an SJW creates multiple accounts in order to pretend to be different individuals and create the false impression that more people support his position than actually do. It is also used to get around site bans by SJW trolls. SJWs never seem to realize that writing styles not only tend to be distinct and readily identifiable, but that presenting the same arguments for the same positions tends to be an obvious tell. At Vox Popoli, we've had a number of SJW trolls over the years, and it has gotten to the point that the VFM and other longtime readers can identify them by as few as two sentences. On the organizational level, this is known as *Astroturfing*.

The Amused Spectator: SJWs love to claim that everyone is laughing at their opponent. This is because they are prone to psychological projection, and because they are low on the socio-sexual hierarchy, they are absolutely terrified of anyone laughing at them. They like to pose as being amused, world-weary sophisticates, but they can never maintain that for long once people start mocking them, and the pose often collapses in an entertaining, rage-filled meltdown.

The Brushfire: If an SJW feels he is losing the upper hand, he will not infrequently attempt to burn down the discussion with distractions, inanities, vulgarities, and obscenities in order to avoid taking a kill shot, or at least to prevent third parties from noticing his defeat. This is similar to how SJWs will always choose to destroy a converged organization rather than relinquish control.

The Crowd Inflation: SJWs always, always, always exaggerate their numbers and posture as if their position is the standard, accepted, mainstream one, no matter how obviously untrue that is. When pressed on the falsity of their stance, they will so readily resort to appealing to temporal bias that the Alt-Right openly mocks this tactic as The Current Year. *Example:* "How can you still believe that? It's 2017?"

The Predicted Demise: An SJW will frequently affect sadness over the inevitable downfall of his opponent, who is fated for certain failure due to his crimethink and ineptitude. *Example:* "It's a little sad, actually. You're really overestimating how much people care."

The Worst Possible Assumption: An SJW will consistently assign the worst possible meaning to every statement and preemptively take offense at it without making any attempt to determine whether any offense was intended or not. This is not due to the SJW being particularly sensitive or thin-skinned, nor is it a case of a mistaken assumption, but a purposeful tactic designed to keep potential opponents off balance and afraid to confront the SJW over his nonsense. *Example:* "What do you mean by calling me 'she'? Did you just assume my gender?"

The Concerned Supporter: This shows up every election cycle, when obvious Democrats claim to have voted for every Republican candidate for President except the current one, because he has gone too far. This is obviously nonsensical; not one single person who voted for Ronald Reagan refused to vote for Mitt Romney, John McCain, or Donald Trump because any of the latter were too *conservative* for them. Closer to home, we recently had an SJW combine this tactic with The Sock Puppet in an attempt to demoralize supporters of the *Alt★Hero* campaign by quoting his own mathematical evidence posted elsewhere to prove why the comics being funded there could never be produced.

Organizational Tactics

The Skin Carcass: Identify a respected institution. Kill it. Gut it. Wear its carcass as a skin suit, demanding respect. This observation is courtesy of David Burge, on Twitter as @iowahawkblog.

Speaking of The Skin Carcass, a reader sent in an anecdote from a friend who, while on recent pilgrimage, had a conversation with someone who is very close to some of the liberal religious orders in the Roman Catholic Church. His acquaintance told him, in no uncertain terms, that many members of the religious orders in serious decline are actually happy that their orders are dying out because they hate the Church and their own orders because they believe them to be unjust. These aging SJW infiltrators not only do not lament that their orders have few individuals with vocations to replace them, but they actively, consciously, drive away any young people who come inquiring, because they consider joining a religious order of any kind to be a waste of their life. They literally want the Roman Catholic Church to die with them.

The Pharisee Gambit: The SJWs inside the organization load an organization's rules and operating procedures with conflicting requirements and procedural logjams. This makes it highly difficult or impossible to get anything done. They attribute the resulting inability to accomplish anything on those within the organization they want to discredit:

The Code of Conduct: Modifying the organization's rules and rendering them more nebulous in order to allow the prosecution or defense of any member, according to their perceived support for social justice.

Unlocking the Door: Relaxing the organization's standards enough to permit unqualified entryists to enter the organization.

The Conspiracy: If you put two SJWs in the same room, they will find each other and organize a secret mailing list designed to coordinate attacks on people and ultimately converge the institution by sundown.

Break the Norms: Constantly violate the social rules that dictate the avoidance of political and religious matters in order to stir up conflict inside the organization.

Blame History Game: Infiltrate, capture, and converge an organization, then blame all the resulting failures on the organization's non-SJW positions prior to the changes you have made.

An SJW Infiltration in Action

Robert Rosario is a veteran Linux and open source programmer who is involved in a number of open source projects. A strong critic of codes of conduct for open source projects, and the author of the Code of Merit, a meritocratic approach to project management and discussions, in 2015 he defeated an attempt by an SJW entryist to impose a code of conduct on the Awesome-Django project. It is a useful illustration of the way in which the entryists surreptitiously go about their insidious efforts.

The attack began, as such attacks often do, with a seemingly friendly and helpful suggestion from the SJW:

> *great project!! I have one observation and a suggestion. I noticed you have rejected some pull requests to add some good django libraries and that the people submitting those pull requests are POCs (People of Color). As a suggestion I recommend adopting the Contributor Code of Conduct (http://contributor-covenant.org) to ensure everybody's contributions are accepted regarless of their sex, sexual orientation, skin color, religion, height, place of origin, etc, etc, etc. As a white straight male and lead of this trending repository, your adoption of this Code of Conduct will send a loud and clear message that inclusion is a primary objective of the Django community and of the software development community in general. D.*

A few things about this. First, the name that was provided is generic and almost certainly a false identity. Second, this comment is literally the SJW's first contribution to the project. Third, while the SJW uses the correct terminology, he offers no evidence whatsoever for his claims. Fourth, his claim that the people whose pull requests were rejected are People of Colour are almost certainly fictitious given that he clearly doesn't know that the individual he is addressing is from Puerto Rico.

Fortunately, Rosario immediately recognizes the nature of the stealth attack. While he politely addresses the nominal suggestions, he makes it clear that the project is not a soft target and conclusively shuts down the SJW's line of entry

> *The pull request was rejected not the person. Of the people who did not had their patches accepted at least one submitted another pull request and was accepted or are contributors in my other repositories, disproving your basic premise.*

> *There is no need for a code of conduct, there hasn't been a conduct related incident with the repository and nothing about a contributor comes into play when rejecting or accepting a patch (as proved above). An explanation is provided when a patch is rejected, and some have been left open to re-asses in a future time.*

> *I'm not white and please don't make any other assumptions about me, they hold no relevance to the matter at hand.*

> *I already work on several projects that hold inclusion as one of their primary goals.*

> *I'm closing this issue based on the explanations given.*

He's polite, firm, and uncompromising. His precise wording allows for just a little more wiggle room than might be ideal, but it is a strong and effective response, especially the implication that inclusion is not a primary goal of this particular project. Perhaps due to the perceived wiggle room, the SJW tries again.

> *You seem to have taken personal issue with well the issue :) I opened this issue not to attack you or your decisions, but to help improve*

a part of the project in which it seemed lacking. Most projects on Github have adopted the Contributor Covenant or a variant of it. It is a very straight forward document that protects all parties, I don't understand your negative attitude towards that philosophy. You may not be "white" [in your profile picture you sure seem white :)] but you are not a woman or a trans-gendered person so you can't possibly understand what they go through (harassment, exclusion, threats) and why a code of conduct is necessary. Even the Django Software Foundation has adopted one to protect it's future, for me it's very obvious Django related projects would naturally follow suite and adopt the same if not similar Code of Conducts. I urge you to reconsider for the good and future of this project ;) Thank you

Now the rhetorical gloves start to come off. The SJW begins with a classic Gamma tell—"you seem"—tries to play on Rosario's potential insecurities and emotions, then throws out an appeal to the herd animal instinct before issuing an implicit threat. The code of conduct is now declared "necessary" in order to protect the future of the project, which is twice brought up in a mildly threatening manner. Notice that the SJW simply ignores the fact that his original concerns were already addressed, thereby negating any need for the requested code. He simply moves the goalposts and proceeds to stronger rhetorical tactics. This clearly shows why dialectical arguments are totally useless when dealing with SJWs: they simply ignore the effective ones.

Rosario responds and again refuses to back down or give any ground:

1- You opened an issue to raise concern about the relationship of a contributor's race and the rejection of their patches.
2- Only I can accept or reject patches in this repository.
You made it clear who this was about.
Apart from this issue, we've had no conduct problems, so no need for a code of conduct.
I'm very certain of my race: I'm Latino, Puertorican, a Mestizo from

a Castiza mother and a Mulato father. There are many more races than just black and white. Yes, I'm not a woman or a transgendered individual and I don't intend to even try to understand what they have to put up with, never said that. But you assume women and transgendered individual are the only targets of harassment, exclusion and threats.

English is not my first language and I hope I'm mistaken but your last line "I urge you to reconsider for the good and future of this project :)" sounded like a threat, please clarify.

This response is overly long and too dialectic in nature. Remember, rhetoric has ZERO informational content, so responding to the feigned issues raised serves no purpose unless one is doing it to expose pseudo-dialectic on behalf of any onlookers. However, expecting a programmer to not respond in a comprehensive manner to the issues raised is rather like expecting sight hounds not to chase running rabbits, so it's harmless enough. What is more important is the way Rosario calls out the SJW for his implicit threats, and better yet, the way in which he requests clarification. In doing so he causes the unsettled SJW to unmask completely and show his fangs.

I really have no idea why you are responding the way you are! Really!! Code of Conducts are not JUST about conduct,they cover all the spectrum of behaviours expected from civilized human beings that are more and more absend in the software industry. You are evading the topic at hand and I can only wonder why, why deny equal opportunity for all to join and contribute to your project Roberto?

That you have not "seen" harassment doesn't mean it is not happening all around us. And turning a blind eye makes it worst. I was not threaning you, but your reaction is a projection of your feelings and now I feel threated by you. Reading the links you posted I only have one thing to say to you: reevaluate your actions,you are becoming a toxic individual who is harming the Python and Django communities and haven't even realized it yet. You are a member of the Django Software Foundation and are supposed to be setting the example. I will be forwarding the content of this issue to the Chair to evaluate your continued presence in the DSF. best regards.

And there you have it. It's all there. Naked threats, point-and-shriek, playing the victim, false accusations, and the inevitable appeal to the amenable authority. The SJW clearly demonstrates that he will try to destroy the project rather than permit it to continue unmolested if it cannot be captured and forcibly submitted to the SJW Narrative. Robert Rosario's response to the Awesome-Django project infiltrator was the best one I have seen in technology yet, as he not only conclusively defeated the infiltrator but exposed the SJW for the insidious lunatic that he is in the process.

SJW convergence is not a joke. These people are genuinely dangerous and will destroy everything they touch. Resist them. Expose them. Seek them out in your own organizations, hunt them down and root them out.

SJW delenda est.

Chapter 7

Understanding the SJW Mind

Individuals who accuse others of unethical behavior can derive significant benefits. Compared to individuals who do not make accusations, accusers engender greater trust and are perceived to have higher ethical standards... we find that accusations have significant interpersonal consequences. In addition to harming accused targets, accusations can substantially benefit accusers.

—"Holding People Responsible for Ethical Violations:
The Surprising Benefits of Accusing Others",
Jessica A. Kennedy and Maurice E. Schweitzer

In my previous book on SJWs, I wrote that it was not my purpose to try to define or understand SJWs, because knowing everything there is to know about bears doesn't do you any good when you find yourself nose to nose with a hungry one. First things first, after all; survival was the goal of *SJWs Always Lie*. However, if one wishes to develop an effective model to predict and anticipate a bear's behavior, then it is useful to understand how and why bears behave the way they do. Therefore, if we are to try to understand why SJWs lie, why they double down, and why they project, it is necessary to delve a little deeper into the SJW mind. It is necessary to look a little more closely at the ways in which SJW psychology relates to SJW behavioral patterns, and hopefully, this will help us understand why it is that SJWs do what we have learned they tend to do.

Now, it is still true that whatever went into making the SJW with whom you are acquainted most likely happened decades before you ever met him, and you can be certain that there is absolutely no way you are going to undo the consequences of years of psychological aberrancy through facts, reason, or sympathy. But understanding why he does what he does, and how he habitually reacts to various stimuli, can help you build a predictive model that goes well beyond anticipating the customary SJW dishonesty. It's useful to know that someone is lying, but it is even more useful to know, in advance, when he is going to lie, how he is going to lie, and how he is going to react when he is called out for lying.

To return to the bear motif, it is useful to know that one should avoid bears. But it is even more useful to know enough about bears to be able to anticipate where the bears are going to be ahead of time so that you can avoid the accidental risk of running into one. And to do that, we need to understand what it is the bear wants, why he wants it, and where he usually goes to obtain it. In the case of bears, the primary answer is food.

But what do SJWs want? The obvious answer is "social justice". That's what the SJW is fighting for, right? But in this case, the obvious answer is incorrect, obviously, because no amount of success ever satisfies the SJW. No sooner had courts ruled that "gay marriage" was legal than the crusade for "transgender bathrooms" was launched. The Narrative is constantly changing. Society's mores are constantly changing. What is deemed normal is in constant flux. What is deemed good and right and true is not what was deemed good and right and true only a few years ago.

There are two primary explanations for why SJWs behave the way they do. One is based on evolutionary psychology and neuroscience. The other is based on group dynamics and social interaction. But there is no contradiction between them. In fact, the two theories tend to bolster each other rather than compete with each other, and taken together, they provide a deeper understanding of the madness, anger, and fear that provides the psychological foundation for the mind of the social justice warrior.

The Psychological Explanation for the SJW

Although his work is primarily more focused on the ideological Left in general, and malignant narcissists in particular, the author named the Anonymous Conservative has written two of the more important books on SJWs. While I do not subscribe to evolutionary psychology per se, for anthropological reasons, the insights of its proponents concerning human behavior are often invaluable regardless of whether they are correct about the causal relationships or not. In other words, evolutionary psychologists are often very good when describing the *what*, as well as the *what comes next*, even if their explanations for the *why* are often nothing more than science-flavored historical fiction. If you happen to be curious about why I am an evopsych skeptic, I would encourage you to read anthropologist C.R. Hallpike's book *Do We Need God to Be Good?*, which demolishes any reasonable probability of a factual basis for the historical conclusions of evolutionary psychology without saying anything at all about its utility today.

And that utility, as described in *The Evolutionary Psychology Behind Politics*, is considerable indeed. In an age where we tend to regard the scientific method as the font of all knowledge, we often forget that our ancestors made a regular habit of successfully making use of many concepts and properties without ever even attempting to understand their core nature. The ancient Greeks, Egyptians, and Indians all used crude forms of antibiotics, and the army of the Sri Lankan king Dutugemunu were known to have prepared cakes prior to their campaigns for medicinal purposes more than 2,000 years before Alexander Fleming identified and understood the nature of the relationship between bread mold and penicillin. When it comes to the brain and the mind, we may not understand why things work the way they do, but we can observe the way in which they appear to work and derive practical information from those observations.

The Anonymous Conservative relies heavily upon a conceptual model of natural selection theory developed by the famous ecologists Robert MacArthur and E.O. Wilson in 1970. Based on their work on island ecosystems, they observed that most species utilized one of two primary breeding strategies, which they named r/selection and K/selection. This r/K selection theory posits that there is a trade-off between quantity and quality when it comes to the offspring of a species. They theorized that, depending upon the environment, it could be more advantageous to have fewer offspring with more parental investment or more offspring with less parental investment.

Species that pursue an r/selection strategy have more offspring, and the parents invest relatively little time and effort into their upbringing. Rabbits are an example of an r/selected mammal, which matures quickly, breeds frequently, and rapidly produces many offspring. The species that pursue a K/selection strategy have fewer offspring and the parents invest considerably more time and effort into their upbringing. Both wolves and humans are examples of K/selected mammals, as they take years to mature, don't breed as often, and don't produce very many offspring. Prey animals tend to be r/selected while predators tend to be K/selected.

The terms are applied to humans in a comparative sense rather than a literal one; relative to rabbits or salmon, all humans are K/selected. But in relative terms, it is easy to observe that some humans orient towards a more r/selected strategy than others; there is a massive difference in selection strategy between a monogamous couple raising four children and homeschooling them for a combined 48 years and the professional athlete who fathers 9 different children on 9 different women and doesn't even know any of their names. The important connection that Anonymous Conservative has made is to observe that these differences in selection strategies have tremendous consequences for the societies in which they play out.

We are a society with such a high level of free resources that we are tripping biological switches in many of our citizens, shifting their reproductive strategy to the r-selected reproductive strategy of the rabbit. Highly sexed and single parented, with individualistic females who seek self-sufficiency and view rearing as unrewarding, and hedonistic men who are unwilling to sacrifice or risk. These are consuming rabbits, and not producing, pack-oriented, K-selected wolves. Nature and evolution put these programmed psychologies in us because they worked well in nature, adapting our reproductive behavior to resource levels, but they are all hell on a functioning society. The problem is, the rabbits as a whole don't produce sufficient resources to keep the party fueled, nor do they care enough about their pack to try. Start a war on poverty by handing out more free cheese and the number of single mom'd households will explode, and they will tend to remain in poverty, even with free food and housing to allow them to continue to multiply. As this number of r-selected consumers grows relative to the producers, it will inevitably trigger the return-by-force of resource restriction and K-selection.

—"r/K Selection and the Wolves and Rabbits of Politics",
Anonymous Conservative

In other words, one consequence of being at the tail end of the biggest expansions of global wealth and longest periods of relative peace in history is an observable shift in reproductive strategies on the part of many people living in Western societies. In the United States, this shift can be seen by the massive increase in the number of children born out of wedlock, which since 1950 has risen by a factor of 10 for all races, and from 2.5 percent to 29 percent for white Americans. This has happened for a variety of reasons that are not relevant to this book, but taken in whole, clearly reflect a tremendous reduction in the average investment that parents are making in their children. While there has been considerable amount of discussion and more than a few scientific studies about the effect that these rising illegitimacy rates have had on poverty, crime, and educational outcomes, there has been relatively little recognition of them as a fundamental change in reproductive strategies, much less the psychological, neurological, and socio-sexual effects of these changes on the offspring produced by them.

What is remarkable about the application of selection strategy theory to human society is that it tends to operate very well as a sociological predictive model, which is rather surprising because it has largely failed to be useful in the field of biology where it was first developed. However, taken in concert with neurobiology, particularly as it relates to a portion of the human brain known as the amygdala, selection strategy begins to provide us with at least a glimmering of understanding of what lies beneath the behavior of the social justice warrior.

> *The amygdala is a brain structure most commonly described as being responsible for the generation of fear. This definition is incomplete, however. The amygdala is primarily responsible for assigning emotional significance to encountered perceptions. What that means is that the amygdala essentially scans all incoming information and flags the information that it deems as important. Likely due to this, it is also strongly associated with the ability to perceive threat, and it is this which leads many to say that it is responsible for the production of fear…. When examining the amygdala's role in political ideology, it is important to understand this structure's purpose and operation. The amygdala provides what is called an aversive stimulus. This is an uncomfortable neurological sensation designed to both draw attention to what precipitates it, and motivate one to take actions which will shut it off by addressing the precipitating stimulus.*

In essence, the amygdala motivates a normal person to alter their environment, in such a way that the amygdala no longer perceives the offending stimulus. Once the environment has been altered to remove the offending stimulus, the amygdala will lift the aversive stimulus, and allow you to proceed. To use the individual who fell through the ice as an example, once his amygdala was trained to cue in on breaking ice, and associate it will the agony of dropping into cold water, it motivated him (with aversive stimulus) to never let ice break beneath him again.

Activation of this aversive stimulus is conditioned, through being exposed to an event, and then suffering a negative outcome immediately following it. The more sudden and negative (read traumatic) the outcome, the more the amygdala will flag the preceding piece of information as significant. If it is ever encountered again, you will pay attention to it, and prepare to deal with the negative event which follows it, because your amygdala will apply a psychologically uncomfortable aversive stimulus until you do.

—*The Evolutionary Psychology Behind Politics,*
Anonymous Conservative

The Anonymous Conservative observes the SJW psychological cycle appears to operate in the following manner:

Tell yourself you are innately superior due to intrinsic qualities related to your identity.

Feel bad about being superior.

Feel super-superior for not only being superior, but for also have the moral sense to feel bad about your own superiority.

He asks what amygdala-mediated process could be driving this continual process and concludes that the SJW brain is using the process to attenuate some tendency of his mind to gravitate towards negative thoughts about himself. This gravitation towards negativity can be the result of physical or mental inferiority, childhood trauma, abuse, failure, depression, or any number of reasons, but regardless of the reason, SJWs find these negative thoughts to be cognitively painful. When forced to face this pain, their brain runs through the usual routine in order to reduce the angst they feel and replace it with a newly charged feeling of superiority. This is why both the Narrative and the social justice identity are so vitally important to them; it is literally their shield against the emotional pain that constantly threatens to overwhelm them.

SJWs are creatures of pain. They are in a near-constant state of mild psychological distress, which is why so many of them are in therapy or on various psychotropic medications. This is why they are so sensitive, so fragile, and so prone to angry, incoherent rants for reasons that often seem inexplicable to others. They might well be pitied, were it not for the behavior that their suffering inspires in them.

Now, it may seem bizarre that individuals whose primary objective is to mitigate their emotional pain would make a habit of seeking out conflict, much less generating conflict where none previously existed. But that is because you are a normal, psychologically healthy individual whose normal state is not one of internal distress. It is only through conflict that the SJW can generate the feelings of moral superiority he requires in order to drown out his steady state of emotional pain. This is why the Narrative can never stop mutating and why no solution will ever suffice regardless of how perfectly it complies with SJW demands.

It also explains why SJWs are so relentlessly critical of others. In a paper entitled "Holding People Responsible for Ethical Violations: The Surprising Benefits of Accusing Others", funded by the Wharton Behavioral Lab, researchers found that people who accuse others of unethical behavior can derive significant benefits from doing so. Compared to normal people who do not make a habit of accusing others of crimethink and other moral failures, accusers are perceived by others to have higher ethical standards. In one study, it was found that the act of making accusations increased trust in the accuser and lowered trust in the target. This is precisely the purpose of the disqualify and discredit routine that SJWs so often utilize. In a second study, it was found that making accusations tends to elevate trust in the accuser by boosting other people's perceptions of the accuser's ethical standards. And in a third study, it was found that accusations boosted trust in the accuser, decreased trust in the target, and even more significantly, promoted dissension within the group.

In other words, SJWs transfer their own emotional pain into making themselves feel more positive about themselves while simultaneously elevating their social status at the expense of others and at the cost of group harmony. This is why group after group, organization after organization, find that acceding to the demands of the SJWs in their midst inevitably generates more conflict, not less.

But there is more to the recognizable patterns of SJW behavior than that related to selection strategy and neurobiology. We can also learn from the hierarchy of human socio-sexuality, which over the years has been refined from simple pick-up artistry used to score with women to a comprehensive taxonomy complete with a reliable behavioral model. It should be mentioned that whereas the previous aspects applied to both male and female SJWs, the socio-sexual hierarchy applies only to male SJWs.

The Socio-Sexual Hierarchy

When we examine any conventional human social circle, we reliably observe a broader range of distinctly identifiable social archetypes that go well beyond mere sexual activity. And it is based on these observations that I have expanded the Alpha-Beta division originally introduced by Roissy of Chateau Heartiste into a hierarchy that covers the broad spectrum of socio-sexuality. Keep in mind that this is a taxonomy of existing behavior patterns exhibited by men, not a theory of human behavior, and it is intended as a useful conceptual tool, not a definitive set of boxes into which all men must be forced. These hierarchies are both relative and fractal in nature; the Alpha on the high school football team will usually be a Delta on his college team since social hierarchies tend to resemble diamonds when it comes to their distributions. The television show *The Big Bang Theory* actually does a fair job of illustrating the hierarchy, although it tends to permit the lower-ranking men to outkick their coverage to a certain extent in the interest of providing eye candy to the viewers.

Alpha: The alpha is the tall, good-looking guy who is the center of both male and female attention. The classic alpha is the star of the football team who is dating the prettiest cheerleader. He is the successful business executive with a full head of executive hair and the beautiful, stylish, blonde, size-zero wife. All the women are attracted to him while all the men want to be him, or at least be his friend. At a social gathering like a party, he's usually the loud, charismatic guy telling self-flattering stories to a group of attractive women who are listening to him with interest. However, alphas are only interested in women to the extent that they exist for the alpha's gratification, physical and psychological, and their primary concern tends to be their overall group status.

Alphas tend to be considerably more popular with women than the norm. Politically, Alphas tend to be either conservative or apolitical. You will seldom find SJW Alphas outside of Hollywood and Manhattan.

Examples: Donald Trump, Adam Levine, Tom Brady.

Beta: Betas are the good-looking guys who aren't as uniformly attractive or socially dominant as the Alpha but are nevertheless confident, attractive to women, and tend to do well with them. They are popular, and in many circumstances, more broadly popular than the alphas. At the party, they are the loud guy's friends who showed up with the alcohol, who are flirting with the tier-one women and cheerfully pairing up with the tier-two women. Betas tend to genuinely like women and view them in a somewhat optimistic, rosy-hued manner, but don't have a lot of illusions about them either. Betas tend to be happy, secure in themselves, and usually up for anything their alpha wants to do. When they marry, it is not infrequently to a woman who was one of the alpha's former girlfriends.

Betas are always more attractive than the norm, but they tend to somewhat underkick their coverage and partner with women who are a little less attractive than one might expect them to be. Politically, Betas tend to be moderate regardless of whether they are on the right or the left of the political spectrum.

Examples: Brad Pitt, George Clooney, Ben Affleck, Zack Johnson on *The Big Bang Theory*.

Delta: The normal guy. Deltas are the great majority of men. They can't attract the most attractive women, so they usually aim for the second-tier, with very limited success. They tend to resist paying attention to the third-tier women who are comfortably in their league. This is ironic because deltas would almost always be happier with their closest female equivalents. When a delta does manage to land a second-tier woman, he is constantly afraid that she will lose interest in him and will, not infrequently, drive her into the very loss of interest he fears by his non-stop dancing of attendance upon her. In a social setting, the deltas are the men clustered together in groups, each of them making an occasional foray towards various small gaggles of women before beating a hasty retreat when direct eye contact and engaged responses are not forthcoming. Deltas tend to put the female sex on pedestals and have overly optimistic expectations of them; if a man rhapsodizes about his better half or is an inveterate White Knight, he is almost certainly a delta. Deltas like women, but they find them mysterious and confusing, and they are sometimes secretly just a little afraid of them. A very physically attractive Delta will often wind up with a slightly less attractive woman than one might expect; this actually tends to work out well in most cases as these women often initiated the relationships and tend to remain head-over-heels about their husbands.

Examples: David Beckham, Jeremy Renn in the Avengers movies, Leonard Hofstadter on *The Big Bang Theory*.

Gamma: The introspective, the unusual, the unattractive, and all too often, the bitter. Gammas are often intelligent, usually unsuccessful with women, and not uncommonly all but invisible to them. The gamma alternates between placing women on pedestals and hating the entire sex. This mostly depends upon whether an attractive woman happened to notice his existence or not that day. Too introspective for their own good, gammas are the men who obsess over individual women for extended periods of time and supply the ranks of stalkers, psycho-jealous ex-boyfriends, and the authors of excruciatingly romantic rhyming doggerel. In the unlikely event they are at the party, they are probably in the corner muttering darkly about the behavior of everyone else there... sometimes to themselves. Gammas tend to have a worship/hate relationship with women, the current direction of which is directly tied to their present situation. However, they are sexual rejects, not social rejects.

Examples: Science fiction writer John Scalzi. Howard Wolowitz and Rajesh Koothrappali on *The Big Bang Theory*.

Omega: The truly unfortunate. Omegas are the social losers who were never in the game. Sometimes creepy, sometimes damaged, often clueless, and always undesirable. They're not at the party. It would never have crossed anyone's mind to invite them in the first place. Omegas are either totally indifferent to women or hate them with a borderline homicidal fury. Women seldom even know their names, no matter how long they've been colleagues.

Examples: Supreme gentleman Elliott Rodgers, Virginia Tech shooter Seung-Hui Cho, Stewart Bloom on *The Big Bang Theory*.

Sigma: The outsider who doesn't play the social game and manages to win at it anyhow. The sigma is hated by alphas because sigmas are the only men who don't accept or at least acknowledge, however grudgingly, their social dominance. Alphas absolutely hate to be laughed at, and a sigma can often enrage an alpha by doing nothing more than smiling at him. Everyone else is vaguely confused by them. In a social situation, the sigma is the man who stops in briefly to say hello to a few friends accompanied by a Tier 1 girl that no one has ever seen before. Sigmas like women, but tend to be contemptuous of them. They are usually considered to be strange. Gammas often like to think they are sigmas, failing to understand that sigmas are not social rejects; they are at the top of the social hierarchy despite their refusal to play by its rules.

Examples: Marlon Brando, Prince, James Bond

Lambda: The men who have quite literally no interest in conventional male-female sexual relations. They clearly have their own hierarchy of sorts, but I can't say that I know much about it other than it often appears to somehow involve youth, free weights, and occasionally, mustaches.

Examples: Milo Yiannopoulos, Elton John, George Michael

Now, it is important to keep in mind that it serves absolutely no purpose to identify yourself in some manner that you think is "better" or higher up the hierarchy. No one cares what you think you are, and your opinion about your place in the social hierarchy is probably the opinion that matters least. There is no good or bad here, only what happens to be observable in social interaction. Consider: alphas seemingly rule the roost, and yet they live in a world of constant conflict and status testing. Sigmas usually acquired their outsider status the hard way; one seldom becomes immune to the social hierarchy by virtue of mass popularity in one's childhood. Betas... okay, betas actually have it pretty good. But the important thing to keep in mind is that you can't improve your chances of success in the social game if you begin by attempting to deceive yourself as to where you stand vis-a-vis everyone else around you.

But for the purposes of this book, the only category that matters is Gamma. This is because nearly all male SJWs are Gammas. And while that doesn't account for all the female SJWs, one common observation of the Gamma behavior is that it is a consequence of a feminized mindset trapped in a male body, so some of these aspects of Gamma behavior will also apply to female SJWs who are presumably responding to many of the same causal factors.

So what, precisely, is a Gamma male, how do they behave, and what is the connection to the social justice cause? First, let's consider the attributes of the average Gamma male.

- Less physically attractive than the norm.

- More intelligent than the norm.

- Unathletic, often overweight.

- Socially awkward and resentful of social hierarchies.

- Generally unsuccessful with women.

- Passive-aggressive and conflict-avoidant.

- Verbally-oriented and prone to snark.

- Disloyal and socially calculating.

- Deceitful and disrespectful.

Of all these attributes, it is the latter that is the most important. One can go so far as to say that the chief attribute of the Gamma male is the relentless ability to lie to himself and others.

If you want an ideal example of a Gamma male, it would be hard to do better than Pajama Boy, the literal poster boy for the young liberal Democrats, who was featured in one of the famous Obamacare ads drinking hot chocolate and wearing red plaid pajamas with a smug look on his extraordinarily punchable face. Pajama Boy's real name is Ethan Krupp, and he prides himself on being what he calls a "Liberal F—", which he explains is not a Democrat per se, but rather "someone who combines political data and theory, extreme leftist views and sarcasm to win any argument while making the opponents feel terrible about themselves."

In other words, Krupp is a textbook social justice warrior. The two concepts are not synonymous, and yet there is a tremendous overlap between the SJW and the Gamma male.

Later in the same interview, Krupp went on to say that he has never lost an argument, except once, and then only because he was drunk. Even if we didn't know what Krupp looked like or what views he espouses, this ludicrous claim would be sufficient to identify him as a Gamma.

Krupp's statement about himself is tremendously valuable insight into the Gamma mentality, and it demonstrates why women tend to find them off-putting. Krupp claims he combines ideas, opinions, and a tone to both win an argument and cause feelbad. But the truth is that to the Gamma, the two are one and the same. The Gamma's victory metric is simple: whoever can cause the other individual to feel worse about himself wins. This explains why the Gamma is constantly pretending to be above it all and unconcerned with the outcome even when everyone can see that he is horribly upset and wounded.

The Gamma believes that if he admits to the truth of his own feelings, he will lose. This is why he is always creating the impression that something is off about him, because it is. Even more than with the social hierarchy, the Gamma is at war with himself and with his feelings. This is why they often appear to be living in a delusion bubble of their own creation, and why they so often idolize Spock and human reason. They like to think they are beyond all human emotions, because they find their own emotions to be painful for the reasons that were described above.

This also points us to the way out of the Gamma mindset and into healthy Delta territory. Unsurprisingly, the transition from what we now label Gamma psychology into normal male mindset is a common literary theme, or at least it once was before Gamma creators began flattering Gammas rather than trying to help them improve themselves. Face your demons. Face your fears. Look into the mirror and admit the truth.

Maybe you're fat. Maybe you're afraid. Maybe you're hurt, lonely, and rejected. But until you stop pretending the situation is different than it is, you can't hope to even begin to start fixing it.

Of course, this observation also points to the best way to psychologically destroy a Gamma. Ignore his words and ruthlessly press on his insecurities and flaws, no matter how shallow and nonsensical they are. I finally figured out that this sensitivity is why Gammas so often shriek AD HOM even when it's not applicable to the situation. Ad Hominem is Gamma kryptonite. Gammas themselves believe their oft-disingenuous arguments are worthless because of who they are, so if you dismiss them on the basis of their own worthlessness, you are confirming for them the very truth they are seeking to avoid.

So, don't ever answer a Gamma's passive-aggressiveness at face value. Dismiss him, and do so in the contemptuous manner you probably already feel for him. Not only will it unhinge him and help you dismiss his arguments, but it's about the only positive thing you can do for him. One of the reasons, if not the main reason, that Gammas constantly engage in snark, bad jokes, and cut-ups is for express reason of plausibly deniability of being wrong about something. The secondary reason is to indirectly take on men of higher ranks with as little chance of recourse as possible. Remember that Gammas can never be wrong, and so regardless of what happens, he will publicly claim victory and it's all a lot of fun. Of course, the vitriol in his words betrays his emotions and reveals that he is actually furious. Being a Secret King means you never learn from being shown to be wrong. First, the Gamma isn't wrong; second, if someone thinks he's wrong they only misunderstood him; third, if they understood him then it's just a lot of fun and games and he's not being serious; fourth—if people think he's wrong, he's not misunderstood, and it's not funny—then the other guy is a jerk and a bad person.

If all of this fails, then the Gamma slinks off for a time.

If the public rebuke was minor, the Gamma will very shortly return as though nothing ever happened and start a new conversation on a different topic in an effort to distract from what happened. If the public rebuke was major, he will disappear, humiliated, for a long time, perhaps months or even years, while waiting for an opportunity to strike back. Remember, NOTHING is ever forgotten or forgiven by a Gamma. He holds grudges for an eternity and will always seek revenge.

He does this because he cannot be wrong. If a Gamma is wrong, then he sees himself as being wrong. His very life is wrong. It's all personal to him. He holds everything against everyone forever, except for that girl on the pedestal, and conversely, expects everyone to hold everything against him forever. It's a sad and horrible way to live, but if you watch and learn, Gammas are very predictable and keep making the same mistakes over and over again.

Gammas don't believe in failure, repentance, or forgiveness. That is why they never learn from their mistakes, or anyone else's.

A Gamma is prone to psychological projection and naturally puts himself in other people's shoes when it comes to conflict and imagines how he would feel in their place. This is true for both reconciliation and conflict. It is why what he thinks is required for reconciliation is usually out of touch with reality, and why he thinks attacks on other's feelings are much more effective than they really are.

A Gamma constantly relives adolescent shame, bullying, and emotional issues. He likes nothing better than to publicly shame and mock those who he is angry with (except the girl on the pedestal) to the point of losing sight of any other goal he had in mind. If you can imagine the awkward boy on the playground being danced around and called names by the others, then how that boy would treat people when he is a man, and you will begin to understand how they treat others with whom they are angry.

He is a coward and will readily abandon almost everything to save his skin, and the fact of his cowardice gnaws on him internally. Being narcissistically inclined, he is unable to imagine other people not being secret cowards, so he will often talk of being brave while simultaneously accusing others of being cowardly. This, again, is pure projection.

All of this negative, self-destructive behavior ends up sabotaging relationships for the Gamma, including his friends, his family, his coworkers, and even his own children. The recognition of the poor quality of these relationships are not lost on the Gamma, and he will often feel a deep sense of personal disgrace about his behavior. However, since he cannot admit to being wrong, he is trapped in a self-made hell.

In an interview I did not long after reading one of Martin van Creveld's books, I commented how SJWs have been able to apply one element of Sun Tzu's strategic recommendations to great success throughout the culture. And, when I thought a bit more about it, I realized there is also a second element that their deceitful nature allows them to successfully implement reliably without even being aware of it.

The first of these two recommendations by Man's greatest military strategist is this:

> *It has been said aforetime that he who knows both sides has nothing to fear in a hundred fights; he who is ignorant of the enemy, and fixes his eyes only on his own side, conquers, and the next time is defeated; he who not only is ignorant of the enemy, but also of his own resources, is invariably defeated.*

The early social justice warriors knew their enemy, and they knew it very well. They were steeped in Christianity, in the Greco-Roman legacy, and in European history. Some of them were children of the West, some were not, but in all cases they knew everything they needed to know about Western Civilization, both its strengths and its weaknesses. And so they went about methodically weakening the strengths and appealing to the weaknesses, until over time, significant elements of the West were no longer Christian, no longer knew their own philosophical legacy, and increasingly, were no longer European.

But the current SJWs are not what their forebears were. To the extent they are children of the West, they are abused, abandoned, and maltreated latchkey children. They do not know the West, and what little they know they have been taught to hate and fear. They do not know their enemy—we who are the last conscious defenders of the West—and they do not know themselves.

That is why their rhetoric is incoherent. An SJW once attacked me in such a remarkably incoherent manner that I saved it for this book because it was such a wonderful example of SJW non-reasoning. He wrote, "You're abysmally stupid and yet somehow disturbingly malign."

One would tend to imagine that one would prefer one's disturbingly malign enemies to be abysmally stupid rather than incredibly brilliant, but that is a dialectical analysis and therefore not relevant here.

SJWs have to cling to the idea that their enemy is stupid, because to do otherwise would risk harming their fragile self-esteem, but somehow these abysmally stupid opponents are also incredibly dangerous. They can only explain this by attributing the danger to evil that goes well beyond the pedestrian variety and reaches the level of total malignity. So, they choose to believe in a very stupid, very malignant enemy rather than an intelligent opposition. Needless to say, this usually violates the first principle mentioned above, which is to know your enemy. And they simply don't know themselves well enough to permit them to do that.

Sun Tzu's second recommendation that is relevant here is this:

War is a thing of pretence: therefore, when capable of action, we pretend disability; when near to the enemy, we pretend to be far; when far away, we pretend to be near. Allure the enemy by giving him a small advantage. Confuse and capture him. If there be defects, give an appearance of perfection, and awe the enemy. Pretend to be strong, and so cause the enemy to avoid you. Make him angry, and confuse his plans. Pretend to be inferior, and cause him to despise you. If he have superabundance of strength, tire him out; if united, make divisions in his camp. Attack weak points, and appear in unexpected places.

Remember, SJWs ALWAYS LIE. Deceit is not second nature to them; it is their first and most reliable instinct. They will lie when they do not have to. They will lie when there is no reason to. They will lie when their lies are easily detected. They will lie when their lies are bound to be exposed. They will lie and dissemble and exaggerate and spin with such shameless abandon that the average individual will find it almost impossible to believe they are doing so.

Because they are emotion-driven creatures, and for the most part limited to the rhetorical level, no amount of information is capable of changing their minds, which is why they tend to reinforce failure rather than correct it. This is why they always double down right up to the very moment they give up and run away.

This ignorant self-delusion on the part of SJWs is significantly to our advantage. The problem conservatives have is that while they know themselves, they fix their eyes only on their own side and remain ignorant of the enemy. Thus the conservative "conquers, and the next time is defeated." The conservative knows himself, but in his solipsism, he mistakenly assumes that his enemy is just like him.

Because they know neither themselves nor us, the SJWs will be invariably defeated so long as we identify them and see them for what they are: liars and self-deceivers. We have the ability to win every conflict with them, and yet we will inevitably lose everywhere we refuse to see them for what they are or refuse to take the field.

And, by the by, this is why reading books like *A History of Strategy* is so often useful as well as educational. One simply never knows how the intellectual seeds planted by the author will sprout in one's mind.

A Cure for Social Justice

The First Law of Gamma is: Lie RELENTLESSLY to yourself to avoid the emotional pain that will otherwise ensue.

Recall what we have identified as the primary attribute of the Gamma male: the relentless ability to lie to himself in order to make himself feel better. Any information, any evidence, that is laid before him will be immediately discounted and disqualified if it creates bad-feels. Even if he accepts a ceasefire because he has been sufficiently defeated or frightened, he will learn nothing from the experience and will promptly return to the attack as soon as doing so will make him feel better.

But how does this happen? How does a man reach a point where he habitually prefers delusion to reality, where he knowingly chooses what he knows to be lies over the truth? It is a horrific three-step process.

First, let a boy fail. Second, let the boy think or convince him that failing makes him worthless as a person regardless of whatever else he accomplishes. Third, repeat until Gamma. This process is all the easier if the boy has been denied access to positive, masculine male role models. For the most part, quitters are made, not born. When failure isn't an option, then the Gamma will no longer compete, lie about his accomplishments, and become delusional about himself. It's also why the Gamma forever seeks revenge against foes, never forgives himself or others, and is nearly insufferable to be around.

Lest you think I exaggerate, consider that Wil Wheaton, one of the more egregious Gammas in pop culture both in fiction and in real life, publicly stated that one of the defining moments of his life involved being humiliated while playing dodgeball during recess. When he went to wash the gravel out of his hands, he met a boy who didn't have to play due to having asthma. They subsequently bonded over playing *Dungeons & Dragons*. He never played dodgeball again. Wheaton says that a geek was born that day, and so too was a Gamma.

I've often wondered why Gammas are so intent on trying to shut down discussion and silence others. And then it occurred to me that they do this, not because they are foolish, but because they are cowards. If you silence a Gamma and he cannot escape, he will superficially submit. Sure, he's seething and angry, and he'll hold a grudge about it forever, but the one thing he isn't ever going to do is fight you. Physical confrontation is simply not an option for him. And that is why the Gamma is always astonished on the rare occasion that he actually gets punched in the mouth. Because he would never fight, he can't imagine that anyone else will do so. I know many, many men who have been in fights over the years, and yet, in retrospect, I cannot say that any of them were Gammas.

Of course, this is also why the Gamma shrieks like a little Swedish girl being raped by refugees when anyone even suggests the possibility of force being utilized. The very thought of it is terrifying to him.

But can Gamma be cured? And if so, will that also cure him of his attachment to social justice ideals? I think it is at least possible. The trick, we are told by one former Gamma, the make-or-break point is to learn how to say the two things that are terrifying to every Gamma.

The first is "I don't know."

The second-most terrifying statement for a Gamma is to admit that he doesn't know something. A Gamma frequently speaks of having knowledge in areas he most certainly does not. To the Gamma, being ignorant is tantamount to being discredited as a person, so he will do whatever is in his power to bluff, obfuscate, and redirect people so others don't see his ignorance. If a man wishes to escape the mindset of a Gamma, he must learn the statement, "I don't know" and use it whenever it is appropriate.

He doesn't need to say this all the time, merely when it is necessary because he honestly doesn't know about the topic at hand. While at first glance this may seem easy enough, it is more difficult in practice. It's challenging for the Gamma because typically he has already hung himself on his own ignorance by saying way more than he should have, so by the time he is challenged on a point, the admission may well cause his entire argument to collapse. Think about this dilemma for a moment. In this scenario, where was the first error? It was talking nonsense in the first place.

The second is "I am wrong."

The most terrifying statement for a Gamma is admitting that he is wrong about something. To stop being a Gamma, a man must start to take responsibility for his own words and actions. Once again, this is exceedingly difficult for those who are not accustomed to doing so. And yet, there is tremendous power in the words "I am wrong." Those three little words are not words of weakness but of power, for two reasons. First, because they are true, and second, because this truth allows one room for correction and improvement. In other words, if a man never admits he is wrong, he can never correct his mistakes or the erroneous thinking that led to them.

At the end of the day, a relentless dedication to the truth is the only cure for both Gamma and social justice. It is not a path that everyone can walk; many will prefer to stroll upon the wide and easy way to Hell. But the important thing is that the harder path is there, and even the most deceitful, self-deluded individual is capable of deciding to follow it.

Chapter 8

GamerGate Leads the Way

What began as a backlash to a debate about how video games portray women led to an internet culture that ultimately helped sweep Donald Trump into office. Really.

—"GamerGate to Trump: How video game culture blew everything up", *CNET*, 8 July 2017

The ride never ends.

That's a phrase you'll occasionally see on social media, often accompanied by an image of a world-weary skeleton soldier. It's something that the meme warriors of GamerGate say to one another, sometimes wryly, sometimes knowingly, and sometimes bitterly, in response to yet another SJW incursion into video games, sports, comics, or some other branch of the entertainment industry. GamerGate has often been pronounced dead, it is mostly inactive these days as far as active campaigns go, and yet it lurks around the consciousness of SJWs everywhere like Marley's ghost haunting Scrooge.

GamerGate killed Gawker. GamerGate created the Alt-Right. GamerGate elected Donald Trump.

There are elements of truth and falsehood to all three statements. GamerGate didn't kill Gawker, but Peter Thiel and Hulk Hogan would not have pressed their suit against Gawker had it not first been targeted and weakened by GamerGate. GamerGate didn't create the Alternative Right, which had been around in one form or another since William F. Buckley, Russell Kirk, and Barry Goldwater chased the John Birch Society out of the conservative movement in 1962, but it showed the Alt-Right how to defeat the media at its own game. GamerGate didn't elect Donald Trump—in fact, most American GamerGaters were probably more inclined to vote for Bernie Sanders than Donald Trump—but it provided the social media arm of the Trump campaign with a blueprint on how to effectively destroy the public image of an opponent without spending a single dime on a television or newspaper ad.

SJWs were, and are, terrified of GamerGate. The mere fact that two GamerGaters, myself and Daddy Warpig, were involved in the Rabid Puppies campaign was enough to cause the science fiction SJWs to panic and retreat to their safe spaces. Their terror is not entirely not without cause. After decades of pushing around conservatives, Republicans, the National Football League, and even the U.S. Army, SJWs finally encountered an enemy that was even more ruthless, even more implacable, and even more indefatigable than they are. As Milo Yiannopoulos once observed, it's really not wise to take on a collection of individuals whose idea of entertainment is to spend hundreds of hours at a highly repetitive task, especially when their core philosophy is founded on the principle that if you are running into enemies and taking fire, you must be going the right way.

> "Of all the enemies Gawker had made over the years—in New York media, in Silicon Valley, in Hollywood—none were more effective than the Gamergaters.... What I'd missed about Gamergate was that they were gamers—they had spent years developing a tolerance for highly repetitive tasks. Like, say, contacting major advertisers. On Reddit, a campaign was launched to contact every advertiser Gamergaters could find on Gawker's site—and not just the marketing departments of advertisers like Adobe and BMW, but specific executives. If you can bug a chief marketing officer, it doesn't matter that your complaints are disingenuous: He just wants to stop being annoyed... Gamergate proved the power of well-organized

reactionaries to threaten Gawker's well-being. And when Gawker really went too far—far enough that even our regular defenders in the media wouldn't step up to speak for us—Gamergate was there, in the background, turning every crisis up a notch or two and making continued existence impossible."

—"Did I Kill Gawker?", Max Read, *New York Magazine*

While GamerGate is largely dormant these days—despite the occasional lapse into old, bad habits by the game journalists—its legacy lives on at /pol/, which has taken the GamerGate policies of digging deep into the opposition, crowdsourcing investigations, and archiving absolutely everything, then turned them up to eleventy hundred. Their method is known as "weaponized autism", their motto is "/pol/ is always right", and they make us GamerGaters look like Jeb Bush action figures in comparison. Their successful hunt of Shia LaBeouf's anti-Trump He Will Not Divide Us flag is hard to believe, as they used everything from cross-references of airplane flight paths, jet contrails, and constellations to identify its general location, which they finally nailed down by driving around honking their car's horn until the livestream camera picked up the sound. The flag was taken down, and a MAGA hat was raised in its stead. It took /pol/ only 37 hours to find the flag and steal it.

But /pol/ does far more than that. It has identified criminal Antifa members and provided information to the police that has led to their arrest, such as the case of the "bike lock attacker" who hit several people over the head with a bike lock at a Trump rally in Berkeley on April 15th, 2017. With nothing more to go on than some photographs and a few seconds of video of a masked man attacking people, /pol/ used his sunglasses and his backpack straps to identify Eric Clanton, an itinerant teacher for the Contra Costa Community College District. On May 26th, Clanton was charged with four counts of felony assault with enhancements alleging that he caused great bodily injury. He also was charged with a misdemeanor: wearing a mask during commission of a crime.

Nor is he the only SJW to have been publicly identified by /pol/. Yvette Felarca, one of the leaders of the December 2014 Black Lives Matter protests in Berkeley and a founder of the group By Any Means Necessary, has been a target of /pol/ for years, which celebrated when she was arrested for battery and resisting arrest on September 26, 2017.

What GamerGate showed, and what /pol/ is actively demonstrating, is that cyberwar is real. It is not just a cool-sounding fragment of William Gibson's glittering imagination, nor is it something limited to government agencies like the U.S. National Security Agency or the Russian Special Communications and Information Service. It is something that sufficiently motivated parties can do together, and something that they can do successfully.

Perhaps the true lesson of Gamergate was that the media is culturally unequipped to deal with the forces actively driving these online movements. The situation was horrifying enough two years ago, it is many times more dangerous now.

—"What Gamergate should have taught us about the 'alt-right'", *The Guardian*, 1 December 2016

The truth is that GamerGate is no more dead than when the game journalists collectively pronounced its demise on August 28, 2014. As one GamerGate meme rightly has it, "Gamergate was an opening skirmish, welcome to the war, soldier." The SJWs were dealt a blow, but they haven't disappeared. Their societal cancer has metastasized and is spreading. But we are the surgeons.

The Rabid Puppies Return

A lot has happened in the world of science fiction since the Sad Puppies and Rabid Puppies blew up the nominations for the 2015 Hugo Awards. Most people focused on the fact that a record five categories had not been awarded thanks to the determination of the science fiction SJWs not give out any awards to the Puppy-selected Finalists who had swept those categories. I was more interested in a few things that I'd observed from the detailed reports on the nominations that were released after the awards, which, in combination with the final vote, made two things perfectly clear to me. First, there was no way the system was ever going to permit us to actually win any Hugo awards. Due to the rather convoluted voting rules, where everyone's votes are ranked so that once a Finalist is eliminated, the votes of those who preferred it are distributed to the other Finalists according to their preference, we were going to have to provide an absolute majority of the registered electorate before we could win anything. Second, although most observers believed the Rabid Puppies were coasting on the Sad Puppies tails, the truth was the other way around. Not only did we have no need for the Sad Puppies to put our selections on the Finalist list in all the categories besides Best Novel, but wherever there was a conflict between the two Puppy groups, the Rabid Puppy candidate won, and it wasn't even close.

The third thing I concluded was that WorldCon was going to change its rules, because that was the only way they were going to be able to prevent us from dominating the short list in the future. And that meant that there was only one way we were going to be able to do lasting damage to the award system that science fiction's SJWs had been using to deceptively boost the literary reputations of their favorites for over a decade, and that was to create a new award while somehow convincing the SJWs to render the Hugo Award increasingly irrelevant by comparison.

But how do you convince your enemy to destroy himself? As Donald Trump has repeatedly shown, you do it by convincing your enemy that the actions that will harm them will actually harm you instead, and provoking them into a reactionary cycle where each provocation from you causes them to hit themselves under the impression that they are striking at you.

This all sounds rather Machiavellian and complicated, but in practice it's usually pretty simple, due to the fact that SJWs know neither themselves nor their enemies, and they react in a mindless but concerted manner, like a school of fish. Add to this their tendency to project their own emotions on you, and if you pay attention, you can usually figure out what action will inspire them to react in the desired way. I also had the advantage of seeing how the SJWs had reacted in the recent past, and there was no reason to believe they weren't going to double down on their previous reactions.

The degree to which the 2015 nominations had upset the science fiction SJWs can be seen in the rapid increase in the number of ballots that were cast from the nomination stage to the final stage. In 2014, 1,595 nominating ballots were cast compared to 3,587 final ballots, a 125 percent increase. In 2015, after the Rabid Puppies stormed the nominations, 1,827 nominating ballots were cast versus 5,950 final ballots, a 226 percent increase. This increase of more than 2,400 voters was the result of an aggressive campaign by SJWs to ensure that no Puppy candidate would soil the sacred Hugo Award by taking home one of the trophies.

There was much public celebrating in the science fiction media after the Puppies were shut out at the trophy stage, so much so that some of it even leaked out into the mainstream media.

" 'Sad Puppies' campaign fails to undermine sci-fi diversity at the Hugo Awards"

—*Los Angeles Times*, 24 August 2015

The drubbing received by the reactionary lobby's preferred nominees shows that sci-fi's future has to be a diverse one.

—"Diversity wins as the Sad Puppies lose at the Hugo awards", *The Guardian*, 24 August 2015

Song of Ice and Fire author writes that he is glad to see reactionary lobby 'routed', but regrets the number of 'No Award' decisions this entailed

—"George RR Martin 'relieved' after Sad Puppies' Hugo awards defeat" *The Guardian*, 26 August 2015

"Hugo Awards: Rabid Puppies defeat reflects growing diversity in science fiction"

—*Chicago Tribune*, 28 August 2015

Science fiction's SJWs were certain that they had turned back the unseemly challenge posed to them once and for all, mostly because anyone who purchased a membership that gave them voting rights for the award at one WorldCon also received the right to vote in next year's nomination stage. But just to hedge their bets, the SJWs also voted for several changes to the rules that would make it harder for a group of outsiders to dominate the nominations by coordinating their votes. I had expected that they would react in this way (although I underestimated the extent to which we had shaken them, since I did not expect any of the measures to pass). But they not only passed one set of rules changes, they actually passed several, rendering an already complicated set of rules into something so twisted and confusing that there was little chance the average science fiction reader would ever understand them. However, due to the two-convention process for rules changes, the new rules did not go immediately into effect, but had to be ratified at the 2016 convention.

So, the SJWs were confident going into 2016 that their numbers were sufficient to dissuade any further attempts to interfere with their annual exercise in self-congratulation. What they did not realize was that their churlish and insulting behavior directed at excellent authors such as John C. Wright and Larry Correia had angered the majority of the Sad Puppies and transformed them into Rabid Puppies more than willing to follow my lead.

And while I knew that we didn't have enough nominating votes to play for the Best Novel category, which is always the most popular, we had more than enough to target every other category. Furthermore, the SJWs didn't realize that, far from me manipulating Larry Correia, the original Sad Puppy, and Brad Torgersen, the 2015 Sad Puppy leader, those two men had actually acted as a moderating influence on me. As bad as the SJWs believed the joint Puppies' campaign to be, they had no idea what a pure Rabid Puppies campaign would look like. Their expectations were confounded by the fact that while Larry and Brad originally wanted to be members in good standing of the science fiction community, and to a certain extent, had craved its respect early in their careers, I have never been a part of that community nor wanted to be. I am a gamer and a game designer who merely happens to write science fiction and fantasy, among other things. But that is no more important to my self-identity than the fact that I have also recorded electronic music, played soccer, and worked in technical support. So, I never sought nor valued the respect of the professional science fiction community or the fandom that orbits it, which I consider to be little more than a sickly collection of mentally ill sexual deviants.

In short, the Sad Puppies wanted to loosen the grasp of the SF-SJWs on the science fiction awards, and see a broader range of authors and works honored. The Rabid Puppies wanted to devalue and destroy the science fiction awards, impale the SJWs responsible for converging them, burn down the science fiction publishing houses, and build a pyramid of SJW skulls.

Metaphorically, of course.

Because we were not actually angling for awards, that permitted us to pursue three goals in continuing to devalue the Hugo Awards. The first goal was to rally the SJWs to resist us. That was most effectively achieved by putting forward works and authors that they found intrinsically offensive. Since the publishing house we had started two years before was publishing more books every month, and more importantly, a military science fiction anthology, we had a good supply of works that we knew would generate strong opposition simply due to the fact that they were published by Castalia House. I knew that because SJWs always seek to send a message, the more we could provoke them, the more extreme their response would be. So, we put the predecessor to this book, *SJWs Always Lie*, on the ballot as Best Related Work, along with a pair of works about the decades-long pedophilia problem in science fiction, and put me forward as Best Editor in both the Short Form and Long Form categories.

Perhaps the most amusing thing about that is that the two categories only exist because Tor Books editor Patrick Nielsen Hayden, possibly the most influential SJW in science fiction, publicly cried about always losing out to the popular Asimov's editor, Gardiner Dozois, who won the Best Editor Hugo 15 times from 1988 to 2004. A new Best Editor Long Form award was established and duly gifted to Nielsen Hayden in 2007. SJWs care desperately about credentials and awards because they are such tone-deaf mediocrities that they have no idea what is good and what is not. Nielsen Hayden's skill as an editor is perhaps best observed by the fact that despite being Tor Books being the biggest publishing house in science fiction, under his leadership, Tor Books has missed out on publishing almost every single major new science fiction and fantasy writer since Orson Scott Card burst upon the scene in 1983. With the exception of Brandon Sanderson, they have somehow managed to reject or otherwise fail to sign every bestselling science fiction or fantasy author from Joe Abercrombie, Larry Correia, and George R.R. Martin to Stephanie Meyer, Suzanne Collins, and J.K. Rowling. It's a rather remarkable achievement when you think about it.

Our second goal was to illustrate the increasingly ludicrous nature of the awards. I searched Amazon for the most ridiculous science fiction-related title I could find, inspired by a dim recollection of having once seen the covers of bizarre, self-published dinosaur erotica with names like *Taken by the T-Rex* and *Ravished by the Triceratops*. They weren't eligible, of course, but I did find *Space Raptor Butt Invasion*, an erotic tale of a lonely gay astronaut stationed on the planet Zorbus with no one but a male space velociraptor for company, Written by Chuck Tingle, a prolific author who is also known for classics such as *Slammed In The Butt By The Prehistoric Megalodon Shark Amid Accusations Of Jumping Over Him* and *Open Wide For The Handsome Sabertooth Dentist Who Is Also A Ghost*, *Space Raptor Butt Invasion* was more than worthy of representing the best of the SJW-converged diversity fiction now infests the field.

Our third goal, of course, was to demoralize the SJWs. They were already exhausted and emotionally spent from the unexpected need to rally the troops to prevent the Puppies from winning all the awards, and the fact that the very popular Dragoncon convention had introduced its own Dragon Awards only added to their growing sense of dismay. However, this exhaustion was balanced by their certainty that they were going to give the Puppies the boot again when the next nomination period

This misplaced confidence only added to their shock when, in April 2016, the Hugo Awards committee announced that the Rabid Puppies had claimed 70 of the 80 possible nominations, up from the 58 of 67 that the joint campaign had claimed the year before. In the end, the number was reduced to 62 by a series of dubious disqualifications by the committee combined with withdrawals by a few weaklings who still hoped to curry favor with the SJWs, but that was not much consolation at the time, although it did cut down on the number of categories no-awarded. *The Guardian's* tone, so celebratory the previous August, effectively reflected the widespread demoralization that was a consequence of the Rabid Puppies' 2016 blitz.

The annual Hugo awards for the best science fiction of the year have once again been riven by controversy, as a concerted campaign by a conservative lobby has dominated the ballot.

The Sad Puppies and Rabid Puppies movements, which both separately campaign against a perceived bias towards liberal and left-wing science-fiction and fantasy authors, have managed to get the majority of their preferred nominations on to the final ballot, announced today. This means that voters on the prestigious awards will now be choosing from a shortlist which includes SJWs Always Lie, *an essay about "social justice warriors" by Rabid Puppies campaign leader Vox Day; a self-published parody of erotic dinosaur fiction called* Space Raptor Butt Invasion, *by Chuck Tingle; and My Little Pony cartoon* The Cutie Map...

A breakaway, more political faction called the Rabid Puppies was formed in 2015, the year the prize was most rocked by the twin campaigns. After the shortlist was dominated by nominations from the Sad and Rabid Puppies' lists, Game of Thrones author George RR Martin said the Hugos were "broken", while previous Hugo winner Connie Willis pulled out of presenting a prize, saying her presence would "lend cover and credibility to winners who got the award through bullying and extortion". In the end, members of the World Science Fiction Society rejected finalists in an unprecedented five categories, voting for "No Award" rather than any of the nominees backed by the campaigns.

Led by Beale—who writes under the name Vox Day and was once dubbed "the most despised man in science fiction" by the Wall Street

Journal—the Rabid Puppies has been successful in getting its nominations on the shortlist again this year; out of 80 recommendations posted by Beale on his blog, 62 have received sufficient votes to make the ballot.... The Hugo awards, once the watchword of quality in the SFF world, appear to have been utterly derailed for the second year running.

—"Hugo awards shortlist dominated by rightwing campaign", *The Guardian*, 26 April 2016

The finalist votes went very much according to form, as after only two years, we already had science fiction's SJWs voting almost entirely in reaction to us, changing and complicating their rules, and going out of their way to awarding SJW-approved affirmative action works and writers instead of merit in most categories. While were only able to burn two categories in 2016, but we were successful in reducing their choices to X or No Award in 5 other categories. This was, in part, the result of poor choices on my part, as centrist writers unable to stand the heat from the Left chose to withdraw their nominations, thereby opening a spot for the eventual winner.

Perhaps the most important achievement, however, was the way in which the 2016 campaign forced the SJWs to show the public their true colors by demonstrating that what the Hugo Award primarily means is public adherence to the SJW Narrative. Among the finalists who were "No Awarded" in 2016 were: Jerry Pournelle, Larry Elmore, Toni Weisskopf, Moira Greyland, David Vandyke, Pierce Brown, and RazörFist. In most cases, the awards in the categories for which they were finalists were given to people whose work was of observably lower quality. For example, the bestselling Pierce Brown, whose novel was not even nominated for Best Novel despite my recommendation, wrote what was almost certainly, by any reasonable standard, the best science fiction novel published this year. The fact that he was deemed to be unworthy of mere consideration for Best New Author conclusively proved how irrelevant the Hugo Awards have become to successful writers and science fiction readers alike.

For example, the Hugo voters no-awarded a serious literary work about Gene Wolfe, the very same people who had previously claimed, just the year before, that a simple blog post was "The Best Related Work" in science fiction that year. The contrast is informative, although it must be admitted that they did have the sense to avoid no-awarding Jim Butcher for a second straight year. Apparently, Mr. Butcher's writing improved considerably from 2015 to 2016.

Sadly, for all of their totally unconvincing pretenses of delight with it, the nomination of *Space Raptor Butt Invasion* embarrassed both the WorldCon and the Hugo voters to no end. Chuck Tingle's erotic masterpiece was no-awarded, exactly as I predicted it would be. What was much more surprising was that there was little celebrating the fact that in 2016, more of the awards went to women this year than ever before, including all of the fiction categories. I wondered if perhaps some SJWs were beginning to catch on to my objectives, as it was becoming obvious that all four fiction categories were increasingly becoming No White Male territory. The 2016 winners were in the Novel, Novella, Novelette, and Short Story categories were: black woman, black woman, Asian woman, and white woman, none of whom is a bestselling or even very well-known author.

I noted at the time that this development was reliably indicative of the awards increasing irrelevance, and that it wouldn't be long before simply being a minority won't be enough and authors will have to be gay, blind, and crippled just to be nominated. As Martin van Creveld, the Israeli military historian has noted, the more women enter any professional field, the more men leave it. And as the men depart, so to do the prestige and the economic rewards provided by the field. This creates a vicious cycle that both expels existing men from the field while repelling new men from entering it.

My success in helping the science fiction SJWs establish this vicious cycle can be seen in the winners of the 2017 awards. Although the new rules that went into effect after 2016 prevented the Rabid Puppies from sweeping the nominations again, we did manage to secure ten nominations in ten different categories, including *Alien Stripper Boned From Behind By the T-Rex* in the Best Novelette category. I also secured my seventh Hugo Award nomination for Best Editor Long Form, which theoretically secures my status as a science fiction great with more Hugo nominations than Ray Bradbury, A.E. van Vogt, Lester del Rey; Gregory Benford, Norman Spinrad, Neal Stephenson, David Weber, Terry Pratchett, and Iain M. Banks.

This is, of course, utterly ridiculous, and tends to prove my point about the total absurdity of the idea that the awards might signify anything but popularity within a very small and increasingly female clique.

As it happens, the 2017 Hugo Awards, given out in Helsinki, Finland, were very nearly an all-female affair. Sixteen of the 18 winners were women, as only two categories, both TV/movie categories, went to male winners. Best of all, professional grievance artist N.K. Jemisin, the very SJW pet whose attack on me played a such an important role in my awakening to SJW convergence in science fiction, won the Best Novel award for the second straight year. If we can safely count on one more round of the science fiction SJWs doubling down, she'll win in 2018, too, for the third book in her trilogy called *The Broken Earth*, which neither you nor most science fiction readers have ever read or even heard of.

And if that happens, I think I will be able to safely conclude that the walls have been torn down, the fields have been salted, and the work of the Rabid Puppies is complete.

ComicsGate

If you don't follow comics, you are almost certainly unaware of how SJW-converged they have become. Apparently, the needs of social justice demand that all white superheroes be replaced by black, Hispanic, or Asian successors, all male superheroes be replaced by female successors, or at least turn gay even though they were quite literally conceived as being straight, and all attractive female superheroes must be replaced with unattractive variants that border on transgenderism.

And it is worse than you would expect. To be blunt, it is worse than you are able to conceive, because you are a normal, sane individual whose imagination simply does not work in the same way as an SJW. As one critic described Marvel's current business plan, they are selling comics books written by people who hate superheroes to an audience that doesn't like superheroes or read comic books. The changes that the SJW writers have made are as radical as they are unappealing to traditional fans.

Jane Foster (female) is now Thor. Miles Morales (Hispanic) is now Spider-Man. Sam Wilson (black) is now Captain America. Riri Williams (black, female) is now Iron Man. Kate Bishop (female) is now Hawkeye. Kamala Khan (female, Muslim) is now Ms Marvel. She-Hulk (female) is now Hulk. Amadeus Cho (Asian) is also Hulk. X-23 is now Wolverine. Despite having been straight since 1963, Iceman is now gay.

Science fiction grandmaster John C. Wright, a longtime enthusiast of pulp fiction and comics who I suspect will strap a nuclear device around his body and blow up the offices of DC Comics if they ever mess with Catwoman, proposes an experiment. "To those who cannot tell the difference between this heavy-handed blotting out and an organic change to the character, I propose a general challenge: Find one single example of a straight white male character taking up the name and identity of a minority superhero or superheroine, or tell the reason why you cannot."

It's one thing to hear about this convergence, or to read about it, but it is truly something else to see it with your own eyes. Once you do, there is simply no escaping the conclusion that the comics in general, and Marvel in particular, has devolved from what was once described as an original American art form into an utterly reprehensible and relentlessly stupid mound of SJW cultural defecation. Consider the excruciatingly bad dialogue, the terrible characterizations, the breaking of the fourth wall, and the near-complete absence of both action and drama from this "fight-scene" that appears in Thor (vol. 4) #5.

CRUSHER CREEL: THOR? Are you kidding me? I'm supposed to call you Thor? Damn FEMINISTS are ruining everything!

CRUSHER CREEL: You wanna be a chick super hero? Fine, who the hell cares? But get your OWN identity. Thor's a DUDE. One of the LAST manly dudes still left. What'd you do, send him to sensitivity training so he'd stop calling Earth girls "wenches"?

SHE THOR: I care not what you call me, ADSORBING MAN Just be certain to inform your new cellmates that 'twas a WOMAN who returned you to prison.

CRUSHER CREEL: What the?! What's gotten into this crazy thing? This ain't how it's supposed to work! What the hell kind of Thor ARE you?

SHE THOR: The kind who just broke your jaw! THAT'S for saying "feminist" like it's a four-letter word, creep. And also… you know… for the robbing?

TITANIA: What the hell's going on out here? Let ME handle this, baby.

THUNG!

TITANIA: I ain't fighting no WOMAN THOR and neither is HE. Not today at least. I'm STANDING DOWN out of respect for what you're doing. Can't have been easy for you. Hasn't been easy for me either.

SHE THOR: Do not think this means I will allow you to flee.

TITANIA: I'm not asking you to. A little prison time will actually be good for me and Crusher. When we've been out too long, he starts to get a WANDERING EYE.

TITANIA: But just so you know, this is a one-time GIRL-POWER pass.

This is just one of literally hundreds of equally ridiculous examples. I could have as easily cited the panels where the Muslim Ms Marvel, previously so enthusiastic about leading people to the polls, is overcome with despair after Donald Trump wins the presidential election. Or when Wonder Woman complains that while her lasso compels the truth, it can't prevent "mansplaining". Or when the survivors of the Walking Dead celebrate the fact that so many of them are hyphenated-Americans rather than white people. The nadir, one would have thought, was when MacArthur Genius Grant-recipient Ta-Nehisi Coates was hired to write the Black Panther comic and decided that would be an ideal vehicle with which to complain about the gentrification of Harlem. Why the population demographics of a single U.S. neighborhood would be an issue of primary concern to the king and protector of the African nation of Wakanda remains a mystery, since *Black Panther: World of Wakanda* was canceled after its sales dropped 75 percent in the five months after its initial release.

The essential problem faced by the SJWs in comics is no different than the one it faces in science fiction and every other form of entertainment. The specific reason that SJW convergence inevitably has a destructive effect on all storytelling forms, including comics, novels, films, and poems, is that social justice intrinsically requires that certain identities be portrayed in a positive manner that is always beyond reproach.

That is why Titania and She Thor couldn't get in an actual fight: because it would involve one woman being violently beaten by another. Sure, She Thor hit Titania in the end, but only with her express permission. Moreover, Titania and She Thor could not actually be on different sides, despite the former being a criminal and the latter being a crime-fighting superhero, because they both belonged to the same SJW-approved identity group.

This is why there is a surfeit of Code Girls and Magic Negros and Saint Gays on television, to say nothing of criminal businessmen, sinful Christians, evil Republicans, and white gangbangers. In the SJW entertainment world, National Socialists are the greatest danger to world peace despite the fact that the German National Socialist Worker's Party has been defunct since 1945, gays are the most monogamous people on the planet, blacks are a wise and peaceful people, women are more technologically inclined than men, and the criminal gangs of the United States are predominantly populated with clean-cut white men without tattoos who last shaved three days ago.

The difficulty of providing modern entertainment under the handicap of SJW interference can be compared to monochrome photography, in which the photo taken possesses only a single hue rather than recording all the various colors of the scene being captured. Information about the other hues simply is not there. For example, if you see a monochrome photo of a dilapidated house out in the country, it is seldom possible to determine the actual color of the house from the image. Is it brown, is it white, or is it that faded blue-gray that you often see in abandoned rural areas? Not only is it impossible to say what color the house actually is, but even making a reasonable guess requires the viewer to draw upon his own experiences that are external to the photograph if he is to begin formulating an opinion. And it is not a value judgment, but a straightforward statement of fact, to observe that color information is absent from the image, and it is logic that dictates the ability of the viewer to formulate an opinion on the color of the object is severely handicapped.

That is the same problem faced by comics, books, and movies that have abandoned traditional morality in favor of amorality, or worse, the alternative moral standard provided by social justice.

While discerning art critics can disagree on the aesthetic value of an artwork, it would be very difficult for anyone to reasonably argue that a bizarre vehicle with thirteen square wheels painted in neon pinks and greens offers a more accurate or realistic picture of a historical automobile than a more conventional portrait that respects traditional color schemes. Whether social justice argues that patriotism is evil, that soldiers willing to die for their country are motivated by hate, that sex is a social construct, or that blacks are all hardworking, saintly people whose historical misfortunes are solely the result of white racism and oppression, it fails to reflect the experience or the daily observation of most people.

Even worse, two is the minimum number of moral poles required to generate moral conflict. But social justice cannot admit the legitimacy of any morality outside its own nebulous and ever-mutating narrative, let alone portray one honestly. One of the primary causes of the decline in popularity of the comics industry—unit sales are down 25.9 percent from August 2016 to August 2017—is the observable moral blindness on the part of the writers, the vast majority of whom are SJWs. There is, after all, little room to appeal to the reader's emotions or moral sensibilities on the basis of a character's amorality. Indeed, the limitations of this peculiar moral palette are such that it is difficult to even justify any action at all on the part of any character intended to be presented as heroic or ideal.

While the convergence of Marvel and DC Comics is merely a symptom of the greater societal decline, it would be better if they tried to build something beautiful in the ruins rather than celebrate the destruction of Western civilization and its moral order.

But the SJWs in comics don't create anything beautiful or inspiring anymore because they won't, and they won't because they know they can't. If you can't draw, you can still scribble. If you can't create, you can still deconstruct. If you can't build, you can still tear down. None of this is new or even the least bit innovative. The preachers of death call themselves creators, but they create only corpses. Fortunately, in this case, the corpses are only imaginary.

At least for now. In September 2017, a group of industry pros were discovered to have been discussing a critic of the SJW convergence of the comics industry on Facebook. Immediately dubbed Comicsgate, the situation happened to be the inverse of the events that led to GamerGate, as in this case, it was a YouTube reviewer being targeted for harassment by editors and writers, rather than developers being targeted by journalists and game reviewers. The group of comics professionals, which included writers and editors employed by Marvel and DC Comics, were plotting to "posse up" and stalk Richard Meyer of Diversity & Comics, a former Marine, at the New York Comic Con, and threatened him with, among other things, "a baseball bat to the teeth." Also, a pair of reporters for Bleeding Cool, a comics review site, were caught trying to get Diversity & Comics expelled from Patreon, a standard SJW tactic that has proven all too effective in more than a few cases. Fortunately, this attempt to cut off Richard Meyer from his financial supporters proved unsuccessful.

The apparent ringleader of the SJW attack on Meyer, Mark Waid, an award-winning writer, known for his work on The Flash, Captain America, Superman, and Fantastic Four, was clearly well aware of the cultural implications of the substantive criticism being offered by Meyer. His criticism of the convergence of the comics industry was a cause for legitimate concern because, with 41,000 subscribers, Diversity & Comics has a bigger following than all but the most successful series. Earlier in 2017, Waid had complained that "several comics folks are getting accused of 'child pornography' this weekend by GamerGate types," after Gerard Jones, a longtime writer for both DC and Marvel, was arrested on suspicion of possession of child pornography, production of child pornography, sending harmful material to a minor, and distribution of child pornography. Waid's behavior demonstrates that across every industry, the SJWs now know they are no longer able to advance their cultural war without facing determined resistance, and it also serves as a reminder that they are not restrained by traditional morals.

Not even the NFL, with its exclusively male makeup and predominantly male following has proven immune to politicization and SJW convergence. So, no matter what your job or your interests happen to be, it should be clear that you will not be able to escape the pernicious tentacles of social justice interfering with your employment and your favorite pastimes. And it is therefore vital to learn and apply the lessons of GamerGate to your own front in the cultural war because those who are unwilling to fight it are destined to wind up as victims.

The Lessons of Gamergate

- Ignore the media and its narratives. They are the enemy. Don't talk to them.

- All their memes and their hashtags are belong to you.

- Identify their weaknesses and target their income sources. Advertisers are the weakest link.

- No leaders, no celebrities, no shills. Decentralize.

- If you're taking flak, you're over the target. Hit it again.

- Be ruthless, be relentless, and be rhetorical.

- A picture is worth a thousand words. Meme harder.

- Victory is not positive PR. Victory is when your opponent quits.

- Keep your morale level high. Cheer on your side.

- If it doesn't work, drop it. If it works, reinforce it.

- Shut up and email.

Chapter 9

Building SJW-Free Organizations

In *SJWs Always Lie*, I noted that if you visit the Wikipedia page devoted to anyone who has been successfully attacked by SJWs, you will find that a significant portion of their page is dominated by the so-called news of their downfall. It doesn't matter if they are otherwise notable for discovering DNA, winning Nobel Prizes, or writing science fiction novels, the SJWs utilize Wikipedia as a primary means of ensuring that every time anyone looks up information about the individual, one of the first things they will see is the fact that the SJWs successfully attacked them.

How does one counteract that when the vast majority of Wikipedia's Administrators are hard-core SJWs fully intent on using their power to discredit people they don't like, and of whom they don't approve?

The answer, as I suggested in this book's predecessor, was to pursue the strategy of building alternative institutions that will compete with the SJW-infested ones. I believe this to be a winning strategy in the long-term due to the aforementioned Impossibility of Social Justice Convergence; the converged institutions have to serve the interests of social justice first whereas our alternative institutions can focus solely on their primary functions.

In 2015, Wikipedia was at the top of my personal list, due to it being both influential and vulnerable. I wrote, "It is influential because it is the first place that practically everyone in the media begins their research. It is vulnerable because as an open-source project, its current offering can easily be forked, and because its SJW affiliation is maintained by a mere 562 volunteer admins, half of one percent of whom are camped on my page."

Since then, 6.6 percent of its admins have gone inactive, and with the help of 176 of my readers, in October 2016 I forked Wikipedia and established Infogalactic: the Planetary Knowledge Core. Funded by donations provided by the Original Galaxians and the Burn Unit, Infogalactic is an SJW-free zone where people are allowed to edit pages without the constraints of having to abide by the SJW Narrative or rely upon the SJW-approved "reliable sources" in lieu of directly citing the relevant evidence. And because it is not a static, one-time fork, but a dynamic one that is constantly scanning Wikipedia's changes and bringing over new pages and updated ones that do not conflict with its own editors' edits, Infogalactic is in no danger of becoming out of date despite its much smaller number of regular editors.

And while it is far too soon to begin trying to challenge Wikipedia's institutional dominance, Infogalactic is already laying the foundation to become a formidable rival. The Infogalactic team has improved the daily news headlines by adding a pair of Drudge Report-style pages focused on news and technology, has created a new type of Verified page that only the subject of the page is allowed to edit, and has redefined the concept of corporate notability to be more in line with the personal notability guidelines. Infogalactic has even been designed into the excellent new browser, Brave, introduced by Brendan Eich in 2016.

More importantly, the Infogalactic team is building the DONT-PANIC engine, which will replace the very old and very outdated MediaWiki engine that powers Wikipedia and is held together with little more than string, chewing gum, and massive quantities of memory caching. When it is introduced in 2018, it will permit every user of Infogalactic to set his perspective filters according to his own preferences, thereby allowing him to act as his own Admin and to see the version of the subject page that most closely approximates those preferences, rather than the version the admins have decided represents the one true reliably-sourced, SJW-approved page.

Combined with the Verified pages that permit subjects to present their own side of their own story, Infogalactic's perspective filters provide for the genuine possibility of drawing off the greater part of Wikipedia's audience, and in a way that Wikipedia, due to its convergence and its centralized structure, will never be able to match.

As we have shown, SJWs crave eternal conflict as well as complete control, the former because they need enemies to generate the feelings of superiority that stave off their long-term emotional pain, the latter because being exposed to people and ideas that challenge their current Narrative cause them new emotional pain. That is why they can never live and let live, and that is why they will never voluntarily permit rival perspectives to be freely accessible by their users.

Infogalactic is not the only new rival challenging the SJW-converged institutions. In addition to the Brave browser, which is already much faster than Chrome, Firefox, Internet Explorer, and Safari on both mobile and desktop, Twitter-alternative Gab offers 300-character, editable posts and has raised over one million in donations and private investments. Castalia House, which publishes this book, is growing at a year-on-year rate of 336 percent and sold more books in September 2017 than it did in all of 2014. Quickfund.me is an alternative to GoFundMe. And perhaps most importantly, Freestartr offers an SJW-proof alternative to Patreon, Kickstarter, and IndieGoGo that will permit the funding of more alternatives to converged platforms, organizations, and industries.

These alternatives are necessary even when an organization is not fully converged itself because too many of them have proven to be unable to resist external pressure from SJW swarms. Even mighty Amazon has proven itself susceptible to social pressure from outside, when it joined Walmart, Sears, Google, and eBay in banning the sale of Confederate flag merchandise in the wake of a shooting at a black church in South Carolina. This may seem a little ironic in light of the fact that Amazon still sells *Mein Kampf*, *The Little Red Book: Sayings of Chairman Mao*, and *Essential Works of Lenin: "What Is to Be Done?"* as well as merchandise featuring the face of the murderous Marxist revolutionary Che Guevara, but then, incoherence and inconsistency are a reliable hallmark of an institution under assault by SJWs.

But it is important to do more than simply react to SJW attacks on existing institutions by providing alternatives to them. As the American conservative movement has finally learned, the Reagan strategy of trying to hold on until the enemy collapses under the weight of its internal contradictions only works when your taxes are not going to prop the other side up and your children are not going to be surrounded by foreigners and subjected to 16 years of unvarnished social justice propaganda.

No one has ever decisively won a purely defensive war; even Fabius Maximus was eventually replaced by Scipio Africanus as Rome took the war from Italy to Carthage. Survival is a necessary condition for victory, but the two should never be confused. That is why Castalia House launched Alt★Hero, which represents the first significant offensive into an industry that has been an SJW stronghold for decades. Both the strong support for the new comic series as well as the feverish attempts of SJWs to disrupt that support tend to indicate that both sides clearly recognize the potential significance of a successful superhero comic that is openly anti-social justice.

How does one go about building an SJW-free institution? My experience is limited, but I have learned the following lessons over the last three years of building my own and observing the experiences of others doing the same.

- Crowdfunding through donations, subscriptions, and preorders takes less time and provides a much more resilient foundation than successfully seeking investment. Investors are much more susceptible to SJW pressure, as they will be identified and targeted. Advertising is not an option, as it is a dying industry, and advertisers are extremely vulnerable to SJW swarms.

- Choose your partners and your suppliers in the knowledge that they will come under SJW attack at some point in time. I never considered Patreon for Voxiversity or Kickstarter for Alt★Hero because I knew that I could not rely upon Patreon, which kicked off Lauren Southern and Tara McCarthy, and Kickstarter, which has banned books deemed "seduction guides", to withstand the inevitable SJW pressure. This is why I was delighted to be one of the first creators to launch a crowdfunding campaign on Freestartr, which is designed to be as SJW-resistant as possible and has proven that it is the campaign that matters more than the platform.

- Rely heavily upon trusted volunteers who have proven themselves over time in preference to paid employees or enthusiastic new volunteers. While I am not at liberty to divulge the specifics, I am aware of at least three examples where right-wing individuals and organizations have been betrayed by paid employees leaking sensitive information to which they have had access to the media. Whether these leakers were infiltrators who intended to do so from the start or whether they were simply opportunists taking advantage of an unexpected data-bounty, the point is that you can never trust an SJW to behave in a professional manner when he has an opportunity to signal his virtue by striking a blow for social justice.

- Do not accept more money than you initially require to accomplish your initial objectives. Excess resources inevitably lead to feature and mission creep. Chris Roberts's *Star Citizen* is a warning of what can happen when too much financial support interferes with the original mission. Chris originally wanted

$25 million to reboot Wing Commander after licensing it from
EA, a reasonable sum for a reasonable project. When he was
unable to raise the money from various game industry funds,
he managed to crowdfund $160 million from his supporters,
which unfortunately led to such a ludicrous expansion of the
game's scope that veteran game developers, including me, now
very much doubt that *Star Citizen* will ever see the light of day.

• Vet every member of the team, from partners to employees and
volunteers, very carefully. Don't pay any attention to what they
say, go through their social media accounts and review their
track record. Never trust a recent convert. Yes, people do
change their minds, but remember, they can always change them
again. Converts are often enthusiastic, but they tend to lack
both the intellectual base required to defend their newly adopted
positions as well as the experience of withstanding SJW heat. Be
particularly wary of the convert who is just brimming with great
ideas and is seeking any sort of leadership position.

• Don't permit Gammas in any position of strategic importance,
much less leadership. Gammas are often intelligent and technically skilled, but their sensitivity and emotional instability can
cause them to do a 180 and vow utter destruction of the very
project for which they were responsible for nothing more than
having their opinions overruled. Always respect the socio-sexual
hierarchy. You simply can't put a Gamma in a vital position
any more than you can hire an Alpha bodyguard to protect your
wife or daughter; the way in which the situation is likely going
to end badly is immediately obvious to anyone who understands
human behavior patterns.

• Be stoic and take the long view. There will be successes, and
there will be failures. There will be ups and downs. People will

surprise you with their generosity and disappoint you with their pettiness.

- Morale is the key to success in every form of competition, including business and war. Always be thinking about how you can infect your team and your supporters with enthusiasm. Celebrate every goal and every milestone, no matter how small, and don't overreact to setbacks, no matter how big. Remember, everyone is looking to you to set the emotional tone; if you crack under the pressure, they will lose faith in you and confidence in the project. Be aware that SJWs will be waging a constant, low-grade demoralization campaign against your supporters, and never hesitate to call out their lies and counteract their attempts to gain influence.

- Rely upon your volunteers, and when you start hiring, hire them first. They will always be your best employees. I was once offered a job as a lead designer by a very successful game company. I didn't take it because it required me to move my family, but I went through the entire interview process, which was intense, detailed, and very rigorous. I can attest that it was not only thorough, but guaranteed to weed out any pretenders, and included an actual test of one's relevant abilities. (I was mildly annoyed at having to create a new game design from scratch considering my track record, so I dropped an unexpectedly complete game design that was five times longer than they anticipated on them, causing the developer charged with reviewing it to complain he didn't have enough time to go through the whole thing. Yeah, well, they only gave me a week to write it.) But I couldn't complain about the process. The employees they had hired using this method were uniformly well-qualified, smart people with excellent credentials. And yet, none of the teams they hired ever came close to comparing to their original team of volunteers, who remained the A team and were still the only ones who could be relied upon to do the mission critical work. Always rely on those who work for the mission, not for money.

• Learn to feed on the Dark Side of the Force. Many people find the hatred and anger directed at them by SJWs to be enervating. I happen find it energizing and often entertaining. Triggering SJWs is not only a useful marketing tool; it can also be a fun way to enhance the morale of your team that is under attack. When we discovered that the comics SJWs found the character of Rebel to be particularly unsettling, the artists on the Alt★Hero team launched an internal competition to provide the most triggering image of her, the discussions of which led to more than one hysterical outbursts. We haven't unveiled any them yet, but the heavy favorite is Rebel sitting on the back of the statue of Robert E. Lee's horse and embracing the stone general, although I suspect the image of her striking an action pose in front of a waving U.S. flag may prove even more upsetting due to the difficulty posed by the seeming contradiction to binary-thinking SJW minds.

Building SJW-free institutions is necessary if we are going to save America and save Western Civilization. Just remember, vigilance is always necessary, and to paraphrase Robert Conquest, any organization that is not explicitly and intrinsically anti-social justice will sooner or later become converged.

Appendix A: SJWs in Open Source

VOX: You were involved in a large open source project on the technical side. How long were you involved with it, and what was your primary responsibility?

OSS: I was involved as a programmer for around four years. In various capacities. On the periphery and all the way up to having some responsibility for key parts of the project. Early in my involvement, the whole project experienced a lot of pain because of leadership problems. I thought I had made the wrong choice about where I was spending my coding time.

VOX: Was it open source at the time?

OSS: Open source from the beginning, yes. But it was run in the typical BDFL style. That's a term we use in open source for the most common type of leadership. BDFL stands for benevolent dictator for life.

VOX: Like the one utilized by Linus Torvalds and Linux.

OSS: Yes, he is the classic example of that today. So this leadership style is very popular in many other open source projects. But success depends so much on the single leader you have.

So, the project had a good leader, but he burnt out and just quit the industry. It was really sudden. That void caused problems. The incentives were kind of messed up too. There were also legal problems about licensing and copyright that made it so much worse. The project all but died in that period. There was a lot of pain around then and the project was really on the edge.

vox: Was there any code of conduct or inclusivity drive or that sort of thing at that time?

oss: Open source is the new frontier for social justice attacks and we're just not prepared for it. People are just not tuned into this because it has come so suddenly. Codes of conduct came on so suddenly! First, a few conferences adopted them, and then suddenly, like almost overnight, every open source project needed to have one checked into their codebase. And if you don't have one, then you're a pariah. If you don't have one, then you're just not worthy, period. And so, the social pressure to introduce these things was really sudden, and very strong, and was not objected to at all. It just hit us and we couldn't stop it.

vox: Specifically when did it hit your project?

oss: I'm pretty sure it didn't happen under the BDFL leader. It only happened in the last couple of years. Like for every major project. It was relatively recent.

vox: But it was after the BDFL leadership style was abandoned?

oss: Yes, it was. So around that time when we were rudderless. We had people talking about forks of the project and other people trying to convince those left in control to fix up the mess themselves. In the end, some heavyweight Silicon Valley companies who had an interest, forced change and wrestled the project away and set up new leadership. We got a code of conduct as part of that deal I think. But we got a structure that put leadership in the hands of the people who did the most quality work on the code. You had to invest your skill to be involved in decision making.

vox: So, it's almost a pure meritocracy in that regard?

oss: Yes. It was great. You make good contributions then you get
       to act like an owner of it. Instead of appointing one person
       as a gatekeeper, you have a group of skilled technical people.
       And once they've had enough, they hand off responsibility to
       the next group who are enthusiastic and who take the project
       forward. It was just a success all round and lots of fun, too.

vox: Especially because the people you're turning it over to are ac-
       tually, by definition, doing the work and making meaningful
       contributions.

oss: Correct. And so the thing in open source has always been, how
       do you run a project so that the people that it matters to the
       most get taken care of? And that is like an open question. That
       is constantly debated. If you give control to the people doing
       the work then there's a good chance you're giving control to the
       people that the project matters to. Why else would they give
       their time? There has been a shift in thinking about this in the
       open source world.

       Somehow these companies agreed to a flexible system where
       they give control of the project to the techies. Probably because
       there has been a lot of experimenting in open source with these
       non-BDFL leadership styles and mostly they are successful.

       And so there was a lot of maneuvering that had a lot of
       people who were scattered come back together under this new
       collective effort, and it's got these corporate names attached to
       it.

vox: But of course, a lot of those corporate entities are heavily SJW
       converged, and I would imagine they brought in a number of
       the sort of SJWs who demand a code of conduct, and diversity
       and inclusivity, and all that.

oss: They did. But of course we had rules where the most active
       code committers run the project. The law was laid down that

said the coding team owns it. And the corporates signed up for that. And for a while we managed to keep that going and had an independence from corporate or social justice influence. Mostly. There are always good coders who are obsessed with social justice, too, so you can't get totally free of it. But it was mostly good. So the coders reported to the corporates about what they were doing, and there was a lot of respect.

So we were still isolated from those pressures. And we had managed all this time to keep it very merit based. Unfortunately, during that time, the SJWs in open source were hanging around constantly trying to break into this meritocratic system, which they hate because they don't contribute. But they have a strong attraction to successful things and want a piece of the action.

They were able to start diversity and inclusion initiatives and they said it's all about expanding the types of contributors for the project to expand the underrepresented minorities. Completely ignoring that we had only seen constant growth with the number of contributors with our merit system. The growth was so good. There were committers from around the world. Different countries. Different languages. Lots of different opinions. Kind of wild and lots of fun to be involved in. The language difficulties were a big challenge because so many people don't speak English as their native language. We already had an incredibly diverse contributor base. And all of the numbers were an upward trend. I mean the numbers were so good for a project that nearly disappeared.

VOX: But as you're discovering, that is totally irrelevant because global diversity is not the genuine goal of the inclusivity drive.

OSS: Correct. So the diversity and inclusion thing sets up, and they talk the talk about wanting to create initiatives for unrepresented minorities and you give them most of what they want. There's lots of corporate support for this too of course. I mean, we all wanted to expand and it all sounds great to reach more people. But their real agenda is at play. It wasn't clear to me at all from the beginning. A strategy that they pursued from day one was control over the open source social space. They wanted to have control over our collaboration space in order to enforce language rules and steer discussions and even remove people they didn't like. The stated goal is always to make it more inclusive and more welcoming to unrepresented minorities. They weren't coding. Not even helping write documentation which you always appreciate. Lots of talking and feeling but not much else.

VOX: What was the general position of the technical contributors themselves? Are they mostly not paying attention to this takeover attempt? Did they mostly support it? Or did they mostly oppose it?

OSS: So I think there were some leaders. The more experienced ones, that were pushing back because they had been targets before of the name calling or shaming and the usual tactics. They just didn't have the patience for the kind of distraction that was being imposed. But mostly I think the leadership was split between people who thought it sounded good and wanted to go along, and others who ignored it all and just wanted to get on with pushing code.

I mean, if you take it on face value, it has a positive ring to it. If you're building up an open source project it's the eyeballs that matter, and you want to collect as many of those as you can. If there're sectors of the programming community you're not reaching then why not? And the peer pressure is there too because everyone's got these codes of conduct. And everyone is talking about diversity and inclusion. And it's only really on the noisy forums like Hacker News where counterpoints are being discussed.

So there's two reasons we might have objected to these moves. One was that it didn't fit our meritocratic system. But as you know, the usual SJW talking points about meritocracy get rolled out to deal with that. The other reason is that a lot of the people that push these things are not really very nice people. You get their aggression when they rant about needing a less aggressive culture. They don't like debate. Logic doesn't work. They work in mobs, and it can be really intimidating. So you get the hint that maybe this isn't what they say it is.

It all escalated badly. The mobs, the use of Twitter and other places to shame and gang up on individuals got out of hand. The name-calling was the most ridiculous of course, everything short of Nazi. Leaders got burnt out. Some got pushed out. Some just couldn't work out how to please everybody that was yelling at them. In a meritocratic leadership system, you know who to respect. In the main you get to please everybody because there's a respect for all involved even when there's sharp division. You move on because you respect each other. But when you turn up the volume and bring in huge social pressure from outside it's something else.

VOX: Okay, so what did the leadership look like. Who were the programmers bringing to the fore and did they cave to the inevitable pressure to accept SJW leadership?

OSS: Some people inside the leadership team were heavily influenced by the outside SJWs. And we did have a couple of SJWs on the programming team. Not entirely SJW, sort of a foot in each camp. Complaints based on the code of conduct were used to push a couple of people out. They were handled really badly. Even now you won't get a straight story about whether the code of conduct was broken or not or whether something else was going on.

vox: But of course, you understand that's what the code of conduct are for. That is why they are worded in as nebulous a manner as possible.

oss: They are pretend legal documents used in legal ways by SJWs as weapons against people who don't toe the line. That's exactly what they are for.

And so the discussion in the public about this was so confused, and they really muddied it, so some people tell the stories as code of conduct violations and other people say no.

We got personal statements dismissing leadership and talking about how the whole project is a terrible place to contribute. They sent the whole programming team into crisis. All this drama hit the project and key leaders had been removed. And so there was all this scrambling about to deal with it.

vox: Have you read *SJWs Always Lie*?

oss: Yes.

vox: So you know that is absolutely par for the course.

oss: Oh it's total playbook. And I mean, it's like *Rules for Radicals*, the Saul Alinski trash. They are utilizing exactly the same strategies where they attack the individual instead of the institution and all that sort of stuff. And so it's all playbook stuff.

vox: What are the most important lessons that you've learned from this experience, and what would you advise people in a new open source project or a new organization that hasn't yet been infiltrated and attacked by SJWs?

oss: Essentially about anticipating and protecting against the attack vectors they use. Be aware of the way that the SJWs see the world in terms of power structures, and that they interpret leadership, even natural leadership, as power. And they are obsessed by power! They always go after power and they engineer these attack vectors accordingly. Protecting against those vectors is vital. And unfortunately, codes of conduct are one of those vectors. Right now, there's very little going on in the open source world to innovate away from that standard fail. I'd be using some sort of anti-code of conduct, saying, look, if you need a code of conduct to be here, then it's not for you.

vox: It seems it's also important to make sure that you limit management of the project to those who are actively contributing on the technical side, because it's pretty clear that SJW convergence is seldom caused by people who are capable of contributing; it's caused by the people who don't contribute technically but come in at it from the marketing angle, from the legal angle, and all the non-technical aspects.

oss: Especially talking about community. Yeah. It's essential to maintain some form of meritocratic leadership structure where the technically capable are able to keep a hand on the wheel.

The other lesson that I learned from all this is the importance of good leadership. It's kind of hard because you want to base on technical merit but you want strong leadership too. I don't know how you balance that. You know, good leaders are not that common, and you can't expect to hand responsibility to someone who is technically skilled and then have them just turn into a leader. When you get people who have to make difficult calls about these kinds of things and aren't prepared for it they just stick their head in the sand. Make the drama go away.

vox: And the easiest way to make it go away is to give in.

oss: Correct. And you set up a situation where people standing up
       against SJWs get interpreted as being the opposite end of this
       extremism that they are facing from the SJWs. And so others
       want to find somewhere in the middle. They don't know that
       the middle is owned by the SJWs, too.

vox: What do you expect the result to be when a project like this
       is completely converged and the SJWs have to run it? Can it
       continue running successfully? Will it blow up? Or is it simply
       going to gradually decay?

oss: So what's going to happen is this social control thing that's
       happening all over open source is going to constrict the fun
       out of development, which is the reason that people like me
       contribute to open source, which is community built on code.
       They want to strangle that. You can't post memes for example.
       Or there are certain emojis you can't use. Or we can't use
       certain words because it is insensitive to some random group
       of people you never heard of. Even our technical lexicon is
       being eroded.

       They will constrict a community to the point where people
       who are involved start to say, I don't know why I'm still here.
       This is not fun anymore. I'm going to go and put my energy
       elsewhere where it's fun because that's why we do it. And then
       people on the outside who are considering whether or not to
       get into this thing, are going to say, that really doesn't look fun,
       and I don't really like that kind of hard work, and I don't even
       understand the obscure rules about how to relate to people here.
       You know people will look at the code of conduct and say, I
       don't, I don't get it. I don't understand what we're supposed to
       do here. So I'm just not going to go in.

       They talk about making safe spaces. But what they want to
       create is not safe for many natives of open source. There's a

scorched-earth thing going on where you either fit in or you need to go down the memory hole.

So projects will be starved of talent and will be taken over by SJWs. If you have companies involved then they will probably still keep it rolling by pushing in their resources. They will have to put more money into all the technical activities and even start hiring people just to get any work done. It doesn't really look like open source any more at that point.

Appendix B: Identifying Gamma

This is a list intended to permit Gamma males to identify themselves in the interests of self-improvement. Not all Gammas are SJWs, but most male SJWs are Gammas. Of course, this list can also be used by women and non-Gammas to recognize when they are dealing with a Gamma and when they are not.

You can't recall a single serious online discussion in which you were wrong about anything in the past year.

In fact, you can't recall one discussion with any friends or family in which you were wrong about anything in the past year.

When you are having an argument with someone and it appears you may be wrong, your most common reaction, and the defense to which you habitually resort, is to assume that the other person simply doesn't understand what you are saying.

When discussing something with someone, and you begin to suspect that you are maybe, possibly, on the verge of being shown to be wrong, you start to get snarky, crack lame jokes, and generally try to change the subject before it actually happens.

If someone holds an opinion contrary to yours, and you don't believe you have a good defense immediately to hand, you start to look for unrelated ways to disqualify the other person as being less knowledgeable about the subject than you and will sometimes even going so far as to begin trying to demonstrate that he is not a good person.

Definitions are nebulous for you, and you don't hesitate to redefine words in order to suit your immediate needs during a discussion. If someone quotes the dictionary and it disagrees with your definition, that means he is arguing unfairly. Also, the dictionary is wrong.

When you are finally shown that you are conclusively wrong about something, it is personally devastating; you remember the terrible experience for years, avoid the place and the people involved as much as possible, and consider your time spent there to have been a personal failure.

You can't even take a mild ribbing from other men about anything outside of a few harmless topics and will immediately fly into a barely controlled rage if you are successfully lampooned by anyone. Afterward, you will look for opportunities to seek vengeance on them for the indefinite future. This isn't based on the normal male desire to best the competition but upon hatred of the other guy, and you will tend to avoid that person and speak badly of him to others.

In contrast you will sit idly by and meekly accept it when a woman openly mocks you. You consider accepting contempt from women as an expected duty of being a nice guy.

In the last year, you can recall multiple women cracking jokes at your expense, publicly mocking you, talking you down to their friends, and otherwise holding you in low regard without any fear of consequences.

The mere thought of being at the center of a comedy roast fills you with dread.

You think width of knowledge is more important than depth of knowledge.

You are an expert on everything and are always ready to give your opinion even when you aren't sure you actually know what you are talking about. If you have read about something on Wikipedia once, you consider that to be sufficient for your opinion on the subject to be relevant and respected.

If someone says he isn't interested in your opinion you take it as a personal slight. This lack of interest in your opinion means he isn't interested in you, and he probably hates you as well.

If someone tells a story, you immediately have to follow up that story with one of your own, which may or may not be related to the topic, and of course is more interesting, more important, and longer. If you don't have a good story, you'll just say something snarky in response in order to diminish the other story in some way.

You constantly throw out flippant remarks with the expectation that they are always amusing, appropriate, and witty.

When telling an anecdote to a group and someone mentions he has already heard it, you go ahead and tell it again because you aren't sure if everyone else has heard it. And besides, he will probably enjoy hearing it again.

You routinely quote movies, comics, and television shows, complete with funny voices, in your everyday conversation.

You genuinely believe that quoting *Monty Python and the Holy Grail* is the sign of a witty, intelligent, and well-educated individual. The more often, the better.

When a movie or story is brought up, you explain the entire plot and all of the details regardless of whether the people you are with asked for the information or even said they liked it.

You sit out nearly all group competitions because you always have better things to do, and anyway, you'd just rather talk to your friends.

At a group event you never voluntarily take part in any sport if you can avoid it.

If you start to lose at any game, you find a way to quit if you can. Afterward, you save face by putting down the game or the other players.

If someone defeats you at a game or in a competition, you can't look him in the eye afterwards and will try to avoid him if possible.

If you win at a competition, you explain to your opponent all of the things he did wrong, whether he they asked for the critique or not.

You have at least one good female friend and are always looking for more.

You are always willing to take that 2 AM call from a female friend who isn't looking to meet up with you but is seeking late-night emotional support.

You tend to focus on a single dream girl to the exclusion of all others and will spend months waiting for the perfect time to ask her out and planning the perfect way to do it. In most cases, your dream girl is obviously out of your league.

You think women are good and innocent creatures, and those who do wrong or behave badly have been corrupted by the evil men in their lives.

Fixing a woman with a lot of problems is a noble effort, and you are always ready for the challenge.

You permit women to use your old mistakes and bad choices to instill guilt in you in order to get their way.

You must justify all of your actions and thoughts to the woman you are with, usually in excruciating detail.

You believe it is always wrong to fight back against a violent woman no matter what the circumstances are.

You know you could be more successful with women if you tried, but doing so would require being a jerk or a dude-bro, and you respect women too much to do that. It is more important for you to be true to yourself. Besides, the right woman will respect that about you and be attracted to your strength of character.

Feelings should routinely be shared, and others should always take your feelings into account when making decisions.

You routinely lie about small, personal matters whenever you know you can get away with it.

If you see a couple arguing, your first instinct is to assume the man is wrong and that the woman may be in need of your help.

If you see an attractive woman in a bad state, your interest in her is immediately piqued. Now that she has been taken down a notch or two, you have a better chance with her.

You often babble semi-coherently and move on to a new, tangentially related subject before you've completed whatever thought it was that you started talking about.

You attempt to dominate the conversation without seeking to actually engage the other's interest or determine if he is interested in your opinion. You frequently leave people wondering "what on Earth is he going on about?"

You have a serious problem providing direct answers to questions. You will answer five different questions that you think they might have asked, or should have asked, while somehow failing to answer the one question that was actually asked.

Appendix C: Code of Merit

Code of Merit

The project creators, lead developers, core team, constitute the managing members of the project and have final say in every decision of the project, technical or otherwise, including overruling previous decisions. There are no limitations to this decisional power.

Contributions are an expected result of your membership on the project. Don't expect others to do your work or help you with your work forever.

All members have the same opportunities to seek any challenge they want within the project.

Authority or position in the project will be proportional to the accrued contribution. Seniority must be earned.

Software is evolutive: the better implementations must supersede lesser implementations. Technical advantage is the primary evaluation metric.

This is a space for technical prowess; topics outside of the project will not be tolerated.

Non technical conflicts will be discussed in a separate space. Disruption of the project will not be allowed.

Individual characteristics, including but not limited to, body, sex, sexual preference, race, language, religion, nationality, or political preferences are irrelevant in the scope of the project and will not be taken into account concerning your value or that of your contribution to the project.

Discuss or debate the idea, not the person.

There is no room for ambiguity: Ambiguity will be met with questioning; further ambiguity will be met with silence. It is the responsibility of the originator to provide requested context.

If something is illegal outside the scope of the project, it is illegal in the scope of the project. This Code of Merit does not take precedence over governing law.

This Code of Merit governs the technical procedures of the project not the activities outside of it.

Participation on the project equates to agreement of this Code of Merit.

No objectives beyond the stated objectives of this project are relevant to the project. Any intent to deviate the project from its original purpose of existence will constitute grounds for remedial action which may include expulsion from the project.

This document is the Code of Merit (http://code-of-merit.org), version 1.0.

CASTALIA HOUSE

NON-FICTION
The Nine Laws by Ivan Throne
Equality: The Impossible Quest by Martin van Creveld
A History of Strategy by Martin van Creveld
4th Generation Warfare Handbook
    by William S. Lind and Gregory A. Thiele
Do We Need God To Be Good? by C.R. Hallpike
MAGA Mindset by Mike Cernovich
Compost Everything by David the Good
Grow or Die by David the Good
Push the Zone by David the Good

FICTION
The Missionaries by Owen Stanley
The Promethean by Owen Stanley
An Equation of Almost Infinite Complexity by J. Mulrooney
Brings the Lightning by Peter Grant
Rocky Mountain Retribution by Peter Grant
Six Expressions of Death by Mojo Mori
Loki's Child by Fenris Wulf
Hitler in Hell by Martin van Creveld

MILITARY SCIENCE FICTION
There Will Be War Volumes I and II ed. Jerry Pournelle
Riding the Red Horse Volume 1 ed. Tom Kratman and Vox Day
Starship Liberator by David VanDyke and B.V. Larson
Battleship Indomitable by David VanDyke and B.V. Larson

SCIENCE FICTION
Mutiny in Space by Rod Walker
Alien Game by Rod Walker
Young Man's War by Rod Walker
CTRL-ALT REVOLT! by Nick Cole
City Beyond Time by John C. Wright
Back From the Dead by Rolf Nelson

FANTASY
Iron Chamber of Memory by John C. Wright
The Green Knight's Squire by John C. Wright
The Book of Feasts & Seasons by John C. Wright

CPSIA information can be obtained
at www.ICGtesting.com
Printed in the USA
BVOW03s0830221117
501062BV00001B/12/P